JUDSON
CHURCH MEMBERSHIP RESOURCES
For Growing Disciples

YOUTH

Storyweaving

You and Your Faith Journey

Wendell Brooker

Text Illustrations and Design by Julie Baxendell
Cover: Design by Jim Gerhard; Illustration by Julie Baxendell

"I tell you its a wonderful feeling when you feel the spirit
of the Lord God Almighty in the tips of your fingers,
and in the bottom of yo' heart."—Sister Kelly[1]

"We are God's works of art. . ." (Ephesians 2:10, The Jerusalem
Bible).

"After having read the chapter, I laid away the Bible
and kneeling down prayed, that the same light
which shone round Paul, might also shine round my heart. . ."[2]

[1]Milton C. Sernett, ed., *Afro-American Religious History:
A Documentary Witness* (Durham: Duke University Press, 1985), p.72.
[2]From Luther Rice's *Diary,* pp.3-4.

Contents

Introduction

Welcome to Storyweaving! You have made an important decision. You have decided to explore the possibility of a new life as a disciple of Jesus Christ through involvement in the Baptist church.

This initial decision may lead to a second, more important decision. You may decide to be baptized and become a member of the church. You will be challenged to make a commitment to Jesus Christ who gives new life to you and to the church which bears witness to new life. Being baptized publicly symbolizes your commitment to Jesus Christ and to a new life of discipleship through his church.

Storyweaving is a program that will help you make an informed and thoughtful decision about baptism and the new life of discipleship in three ways. *Storyweaving* helps by providing:

1. the *content* of the Christian story and the Baptist tradition in twelve learning sessions with the pastor/leader,

2. the personal *encouragement* of a caring and supportive mentor whose Christian experience serves as a model, and

3. the *practice* of discipleship through guided ministry projects.

You will be encouraged to reflect on what you learn, feel, and practice during the course of the *Storyweaving* program by writing in your guidebook. Whatever you write is between you and God and will not be read by anyone else without your permission.

Please read all the material in your book, ask every hard question that comes to mind, complete the ministries you choose, and enjoy the task of discovering your special place in the great fabric of God's creation. Enter the story of Jessie and Josh now; allow God to weave your story together with those of the disciples of the Bible and our Baptist tradition. This is your printed invitation to new life.

The Ponder Place: Who Am I and Where Am I Going?

The Kansas road was flat and deserted and the horizon was empty on the bright spring day when Jessie's father drove her to her grandmother's house. Jessie's mind and heart were teeming with a tangle of thoughts, images, and questions that were casting a shadow on her day. The questions would not settle down. It was spring break and Jessie was looking forward to four days away from her eighth-grade class and her home neighborhood in Topeka. What used to be a ride to the country no longer seemed so long now. The country had become the suburbs. Even now workers were busy constructing new homes where Grampa used to farm.

Jessie's father tried asking her how she felt as they rode along, but she just couldn't share anything with her parents these days. "Parents just don't understand," she thought to herself. She told her father that she was trying to hear the song on the car radio. His eyes were hurt but his lips stayed buttoned. Jessie's mind kept working, grinding away at the questions that wouldn't quit.

The class with the pastor had started innocently enough. He was a voice on the phone one day asking if she had given any thought to being baptized and joining the church. Of course she hadn't; nothing could possibly have been farther from her mind. But it was a dark, dreary day two weeks after Christmas and her best friend, Jeri, had just moved to Texas. Her life was kind of up in the air and so something told her to say yes. Maybe there would be a new friend in the class. It was unlikely, but possible.

Actually, it had suddenly intrigued her that she was not a member of the church. The church had always been there, as long as she could remember. Mail from the church had been as certain as homework, and every three or four months Jessie's mother would go through a hysterical guilt trip and make everyone go to church for a week or two until real life got back in the way again. What did it mean to be a "member" of the church if she wasn't? Was she missing something? Twelve weeks seemed like a long time, but the pastor assured her that she could drop out if she wasn't ready, whatever that meant. She wasn't doing much on Wednesday afternoons anyway.

How could she have known at the time that she was more ready for that class than she ever would be again?

The crunch of the tires on the gravel driveway broke Jessie's thinking and told her that they had arrived. The old white house, which was almost in need of a coat of paint, pulled her thoughts in a different direction. The sag in the porch that held two wooden rockers was a favorite spot, the "ponder place" her grandmother had called it. Her grandmother had always listened when no one else would and the rockers still marked the spot.

But would she listen now? Could she? Jessie had such big questions. She needed to talk them out, but could she? She was a little worried about offending her grandmother, who never missed church. She was more worried, she decided, about letting this opportunity for "new life" slide by.

Jessie had attended all twelve sessions with the pastor and had made friends with Mrs. Hartley, who was a member of the church and also a Spanish teacher at her school. A "mentor" they called her, and she helped Jessie in many ways with her questions. But now Jessie had a decision to make, a decision that had once seemed unimportant and irrelevant but now haunted her with its troubling presence. Yes, she was giving much thought indeed to baptism and church membership.

The warm hug from her grandmother and the remembered smells of the kitchen made her glad she had come. Her father lingered for only a moment; he had to get to the airport. Then she was sitting across the kitchen table from her grandmother with a Dr. Pepper in her hand, sharing the latest news from home and school. The troubling questions receded a bit as the ease of the moment settled her and Jessie decided that there would be time for them later. Her grandmother was just beginning to share a story from her own school days when the front doorbell rang.

"Would you get that, please,?" her grandmother asked. Jessie walked through the familiar dining and living rooms over the hand-woven rugs and into the front hallway where a bright new wall hanging caught her eye. She opened the door wide and her jaw dropped a mile. Standing there with a big plastic bag in his hand and an amused smile on his face was the best-looking boy she had ever seen.

Respond to the following:

1. What were your first thoughts when you were invited to participate in this program?

2. Are you "ready" for baptism? What does that phrase mean to you?

3. Do you have a ponder place? Who are the people with whom you like best to "talk things out"?

Unit I.

THE STORY OF CREATION

The story of creation is like the story of a weaver at a loom, carefully and lovingly creating the tapestry we know as life, both the life of humankind in general and of your life as an individual. As the weaver weaves, we see yarn of a variety of textures and colors grow into patterns and pictures which finally emerge into symbols and stories from the imagination of the weaver.

God has promised a perfect fabric in the carpet of creation. It is not complete yet. God has created you to be an important part of that fabric. The story of your life is carefully, lovingly interwoven with the great story of creation.

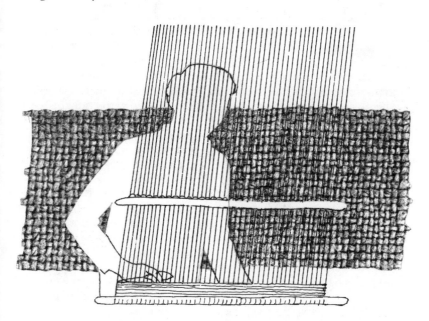

1

The Wondrous Weaver

Jessie watched while her grandmother hovered around Josh at the loom, making sure that everything was in place for efficient work. She made sure he was seated so that the colored yarn could be reached easily without disturbing the rhythm of his weaving and so that his back and neck would be in a natural position as his fingers moved among those strands stretched across the frame. Jealousy nibbled at the edge of Jessie's thoughts; she didn't know that her grandmother had taken on a new student and one her own age, too.

Jessie thought back to her first encounter with Josh at the front door. She must have looked like an A-1 idiot, standing there with her jaw sagging and her hair still frizzy from the windy ride out. Finally, after what had seemed an eternal moment, her grandmother had invited him in over Jessie's shoulder and introduced them. Josh was a Navajo Indian who lived "down the road" from her grandmother. When he had discovered that Jessie's grandmother was part Navajo and that she proudly maintained the weaving tradition of his people, he asked if she would teach him. He was her first male apprentice.

Josh was slow yet, but he was learning. In his bag he brought yarn which he had spun and dyed himself in classic Navajo colors. They laughed as he worked, but once, when he miscounted and changed colors one row too soon, Jessie's grandmother spoke sharply. Together they undid the row and got back on track for the pattern. "How does she keep it all in mind?" Jessie wondered. Her grandmother never seemed to lose count. Jessie wandered into the dining room and noted the perfection in the 6-by-9-ft. carpet. Yes, grandma was "a wondrous weaver." Jessie's grandmother used to call her own mother that name.

Later, after dinner was finished and the dishes washed, they went out onto the coolness of the porch, to the ponder place, and watched the stars come out. Jessie mentioned that Josh was not a very good weaver yet. The red threads in the little tapestry that hung in the hallway did not all match. "Well," her grandma said, "that's only his second one. He's learning, and quickly. You watch him; you'll see what I mean."

"Tell me about the wondrous weaver again," Jessie said, hoping to hear the story of how her grandmother learned to put together all those threads and colors in such marvelous ways from her own mother.

"There's only one wondrous weaver I can think about tonight," Grandma said quietly. Then, pointing to the stars, she quoted: " 'When I consider thy heavens, the work of thy fingers. . . .' Read Psalm 8 before you go to sleep tonight."

"Psalm 8 was one the pastor showed us in the church membership class," Jessie said. Her grandmother looked at her with surprise.

"Church membership?" she repeated and smiled. "I'm going to want to hear about that tomorrow. Now I'm tired and need to rest."

Jessie went to her room and read again from Psalm 8. An image came to her mind of a loom and a weaver, a wondrous weaver whose face she could not quite make out but whose hands were wonderfully quick. She read from her disciple's guidebook about the shepherd David, who might have written the psalm, and about Ann Judson who surely struggled with it. She thought about her parents, her brothers, Jeri, her new friends from the membership class, Mrs. Hartley, her grandmother, and finally Josh. What a tangled web God was weaving! Her questions began to bubble up to the surface or her brain again, but then she finally found herself able to sleep beneath the starlit, moonlit sky.

Ann Judson: A Story of Struggle

It was a quiet night aboard ship, and Ann Judson was grateful for the slight breeze that rustled her hair. The moon and stars were crystal as she considered the words of the psalm, "When I consider thy heavens. . . ."

She and Adoniram had been on this boat for months now but the worst was yet to come, perhaps worse than she could even imagine. Her husband was so honest. He had laid out very clearly for her father how hard it would be, how filled with danger, to be a missionary in a foreign land. Somehow her father had been persuaded to let her go.

Now as they neared their first stop in India, Ann was troubled. Adoniram had taken up the study of infant baptism to pass the time on board ship and somehow became convinced that the Baptists were right. "Scripture is clear," he said. "It's not easy to admit, but I must be honest with God and with myself." He was ready to become a Baptist, but Ann was deeply troubled; she had questions. "Aren't we here to minister with the blessing and support of all those good Congregational people at home in New England?" she thought. "Aren't we obligated to teach their beliefs?

"Weren't we ourselves baptized as infants? Are our own baptisms now to be questioned? How could we become Baptists? Do the Baptists in America even want to support foreign missionaries? Are we to cut ourselves off from everyone and be left completely alone?"

Ann had begged her husband to reconsider, but she had begun to do some Bible study of her own. She had fought his conclusions, but he was convinced. She had searched the Scriptures relentlessly for help.

It was not easy, but Ann trusted her heart to God and to the Word. Finally, it became clear to her also. The decision for Christ must come first, then the act of baptism to confirm it. It was too plain to miss and she knew they would have to follow the truth as they discovered it. She would have to part ways with their former friends, spiritually as well as geographically.

Ann considered the moon and stars again and felt at home with God. She went to tell Adoniram what she had discovered.

A Psalm of David

There were so many nights when David was left out alone with the flocks by his father and brothers. Someone would bring him his meal and then they would all get on with more important things.

But David began to enjoy the solitude of tending the sheep. In the dark nights, with the flock dependent on him for care and protection, he began to feel like an important part of God's creation. The moon and the stars became his friends.

There was excitement, too, on occasion. One night he chased away a lion that was approaching his sheep. He began to feel close to God's creation, as if he were chosen for something special. He began to feel the touch of God at many times and in places during each day. And he trusted God for his place in the scheme of things.

David sang to his sheep and began to compose songs on his harp. And one night, when the sky was its darkest and the moon and stars their brightest, he began to compose his thoughts with a question:

> When I consider thy heavens, the work of thy fingers,
> the moon and the stars, which thou hast ordained;
> What is man that thou art mindful of him?
>
> —Psalm 8:3-4 (KJV)

The Carpet of Creation

Jessie awakened in the cold of the early spring morning with questions on her mind. Her body was accustomed to waking up at 5:45 A.M. but she was glad that the 6:51 A.M. school bus would not appear for her out here at her grandmother's house. It was too early to disturb her grandmother with her questions, and so she began looking through her Bible and the *Storyweaving* book which she had brought with her and placed on the bedstand. The story of Job and the picture of Roger Williams caught her attention.

Jessie turned in her Bible again to Job 38–39 which had become one of her favorite places for reading. Here was God speaking about the universe God had created, and no one could escape the love God felt for that creation. The sea, the snow, the rain and hail, the lion, the goat, the ostrich and horse—God had created and loved them all, in all their glory and peculiarity.

Jessie climbed out from under the warm blankets and walked to the window. She wiped the glass clean of moisture and looked out through the fog that was rising from the earth in the first rays of the morning sun. God's world was just waiting to be discovered again. "Each morning the world is new," her grandmother would say. Jessie could see the newness today. She hadn't noticed the rabbits for years, but there they were, feeding on the clover in the back yard, completely unafraid of the neighbor's old, blind dog who stumbled through his morning walk, concentrating on the six inches of turf immediately before him. Jessie looked out toward the construction site where mud and naked lumber now replaced the cow pasture and corn fields; she wondered if there were still turtles out that way now that the cow pond was gone.

She looked the other way and saw a figure moving quickly between a series of sheds and a barn, carrying bags and buckets and moving relentlessly from place to place. He had no time to stop. Josh's spring break was not this week and he would have to complete his chores before the school bus came. Jessie marvelled at how quickly he did his chores. He seemed to know just what he was doing; he clearly knew his place in the morning scheme of things. He was different at the loom.

Jessie dressed and, as she laced up her boots, she noticed the 10-by-14-ft. carpet in the bedroom for the first time. It began with a classic Navajo landscape pattern of sun, mesas, and canyons, but there was something different about it; it took her a while to focus on what it was. Finally she discovered seven Navajo landscapes, one after the other, moving from one end of the carpet to the other. Each landscape was a variation of the first. The colors were the same but the hills, canyons, mesas, and natural growth were different in size and shape. Each landscape was more complex that the one below. Once she discovered the pattern, the carpet was breathtakingly beautiful. Jessie wondered how long it had taken her grandmother to weave it.

The words of God from Job came back to her.

"Who is this that darkens counsel
  by words without knowledge?

"Where were you when I laid the foundation of the earth?
. . . When the morning stars sang together,
and all the sons of God shouted for joy?"   —Job 38:2-7

"Where have I been?" Jessie thought. "As lost as the friends of Job?" She was glad that she had come here with her questions. Her grandmother clearly knew something about the richness of God's creation in all its varied forms.

She looked at the picture of Roger Williams and remembered his characteristic restlessness. She felt close to him in the restlessness he experienced as he moved from place to place in God's creation, seeking a spiritual home. There were times she wasn't sure she was in the right place either. It would be fun to explore and peek into all those canyons in the beautifully woven carpet. The words of Job came again:

"I had heard of thee by the hearing of the ear,
but now my eye sees thee."   —Job 42:5   15

Was Roger Williams ever able to affirm that? Was that the "amazedness of spirit" he talked about? Would she ever discover it? Jessie cherished her freedom to find out about God and resolved to accept responsibility for that freedom. Bring on those canyons!

A Restless Seeker

A certain restlessness of spirit marked the man who did so much to forge the distinctive style of Baptist spirituality that we identify with the term "soul freedom." It was this restlessness of spirit that drove Roger Williams to leave England for the challenge and rigors of the New World in the 1630s. It was this restlessness of spirit that drove him to confront the stifling repression of the civil and religious authorities of the Massachusetts Bay Colony, who finally expelled him from the colony in 1636. It was this restlessness that marked his famous theological debate with John Cotton and joined him with a small band of dissidents who founded a new colony in Rhode Island, where there would be religious freedom for all under a government that would have authority only in civil matters. This was the birth place of the idea of separation of church and state. Each human soul, Williams argued, must be free to make its own peace with God.

But there was another side of Roger Williams that knew quite clearly that "soul freedom" was only possible when there was "soul responsibility." The human soul needs to be free from repressive human systems of belief so that it can be genuinely responsible to God. Williams argued for what he called a "delightful privacy with God" by which each free person could discover his or her personal responsibilty and call. This deep sense of responsibility to God caused Williams to name the city he founded Providence, after the grace of God. This same insight drove him to see the necessity of the believer's baptism. He became pastor of the first Baptist church in America, where people would acknowledge their "soul responsibility" alongside their "soul freedom." This same concern caused him eventually to desert the first Baptist church in order to search out further truth about God. He called himself, finally, a "seeker." He went to serve as a missionary among the Narragansetts and other Indians in the wilderness of Rhode Island, translating the message of the gospel into their languages. He was free from people but responsible to God.

"Seek, and ye shall find," (Matthew 7:7, KJV) was a watchword of this restless man's faith which has become a distinguishing mark of genuine Baptist spirituality. When Roger Williams defined the marks of "Christian Spiritual Health" in a printed tract, he said the first mark is that "God's children ought to walk in constant amazedness of spirit as to God, His nature, His works."

16

Job:
Awakened to Creation

"It was a real eye-opener for me; one I didn't expect. My name is Job. Maybe you know part of my story; I just wanted to make sure you knew the rest of the story.

"I had a good life; it really couldn't have been better. I rejoiced in it and thanked God constantly for it. And then one day it began to come apart. My property which was extensive was devastated, my flocks and possessions destroyed. Just as I struggled to put this into perspective, my servants and then my children were killed and I was left alone with my wife. And finally my flesh was covered with boils. I was a beaten man. My wife, God bless her, advised me to simply curse God and die. I was tempted to do just that but somehow I resisted.

"Then there were my friends Eliphaz, Bildad, and Zophar who came to see me. At first I was elated to see them, but later it seemed they had appeared only to pour oil on the fire. They were relentless in condemning me and seeking out the sin that had brought all this upon me. I was sure, however, that I had been faithful and finally that somehow and somewhere my Redeemer lived. Then there was Elihu. I never understood what he wanted but he, too, was filled with words.

"Just when all the struggle, pain, and argument seemed to be going nowhere, God suddenly spoke out of a whirlwind.

"God didn't specifically respond to my pain at all. In fact, God seemed more than a little offended at this entire discussion we'd been having. God began to speak about the creation with such knowledge, love, and tender concern that we were overwhelmed and speechless. My perspective became enlarged as God spoke. What a wonderful Creator it was who could weave a coherent fabric of the most minute moments of each creature's life. My jaw must have hung in shame like a broken pump handle. Who was I from my small life to raise such questions about such a magnificent fabric of creation? But then God went further and affirmed even my questions as consistent with the fabric. It was my friends whom God took to task.

"What could I say? The God I had only heard about before had now personally invited me to see. I was awakened again to the enormity of both the beauty and mystery of this creation and its Weaver. While my mind remains yet too small to put it all together, more than ever the wonder of it all continues to feed my spirit. God cares about even the minutest of threads, even me."

Naming the Strands of Your Tapestry

Your life is one of the strands of yarn that God is weaving into the great tapestry of life we call creation. Name some of the other strands God is tamping in close to yours.

1. Some strands are people: _____

_____

_____

_____

_____

2. Some strands are places: _____

_____

_____

_____

3. Some strands are events: _____

_____

_____

_____

4. Some strands are ideas: _____

_____

_____

_____

5. Strands from other sources: _____

_____

_____

From the list on the left, name the most influential and important strands in your part of the tapestry of life and write them on the lines above.

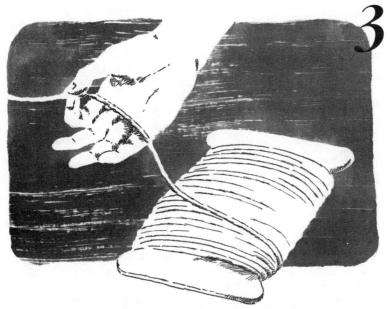

Woven for Weaving

Jessie marveled at the careful, patient work of her grandmother at the loom where she had begun just yesterday to make a new 6-by-9-ft. carpet. She continued to work in the same old-fashioned way, not like the art teachers at school with the power looms. No wonder Jessie had gotten tired of the lessons her grandmother had given her and had decided to give them up.

Her grandmother's fingers moved automatically through the course strands of warp as if they had eyes, working a thread of deep brown over and under, in and out until she reached the other end of the pattern. Then she took a different shade and worked it through as well. "How did she know just which colors would make the finished pattern?" Jessie pondered. Then the weaver kneaded and pressed the weft threads into place with her hand-carved weaver's comb, a gift from her own mother. The batten lay close at hand for when the strings needed adjusting.

"You must have a picture, a vision, in your mind to begin with," her grandmother was saying, "and you have to have an idea of how the colors all fit together and change one another."

"Do you think Josh will ever be able to do what you do?" Jessie asked.

"Of course, once he gets the hang of it. It's all practice. Tell me about your classes at the church; I didn't know you cared much about church."

"Well, we never have. I guess the pastor just caught me at a good time. I've been learning a lot about Baptists and weaving. Our book is called *Storyweaving*. I guess that's why I wanted you to help."

"I was hoping it was more than learning about Baptists, Jessie. We've had Baptists in our family for a long time. I hoped maybe you were finally, really becoming a Baptist." The work at the loom continued at its own pace while Grandmother spoke.

"Maybe I am," Jessie said. "I'm just not sure about a lot of things. How are you so sure about your church?"

"Oh, I'm not so sure as you might think, child. But I am sure of one thing. There is a big Weaver with a big plan in mind who keeps on weaving everything together in marvelous ways—life and death, good and bad, you, Josh, and me and your church, too. It all fits together somehow." Just then the new thread tangled.

"Sometimes this yarn seems to have a mind of its own," she said as she worked at the snag.

"I guess we're even worse for God to work with than yarn for a weaver," Jessie mumbled. "We've always got minds of our own."

"Well, you've got that right," Grandmother smiled. "But let's remember we're created in the image of God, to do some weaving of our own for the Great Weaver. God wants more than lifeless thread from us; God wants commitment, and commitment is rooted in choice, and choice is rooted in freedom."

"That's what the pastor meant by 'soul freedom,' I guess."

"Yes, we're a special kind of thread, free to help or hinder the weaver of life. And we share in God's creativity and weaving somehow. You and I, too, are composed of threads that come together from various places in our own lives."

"In our class, we learned about a black man named Lott Carey. He lived when black people were slaves in this country. He was a man who earned his freedom and, once free, was woven into the fabric of God's big story of love. He was so excited about the possibility of new life that he decided to return to Africa to help God do some weaving in his homeland."

" 'We love because God first loved us,' " Grandmother quoted. "That's from John's letters, I think."

"We learned about Ezekiel and the other prophets and how God used their creative abilities and gifts to weave the story of the Old Testament. And we learned about a theologian named Langdon Gilkey, who explained what it means to be God's creature."

"Whoo, you're getting too far for me now. I don't know too much about theologians. Jessie, I'm proud of you. Don't you think it's time we got back to some weaving lessons, now? Over there in the corner is your loom and there's lots of yarn."

"Well sure, now I'm ready to begin; I'm woven for weaving."

The Prophet Ezekiel

The prophet Ezekiel was part of the group of Hebrew leaders who were captured and taken into exile by the powerful Babylonians after the surrender of King Jehoiachin to King Nebuchadnezzar, in 598 B.C. He was the son of Buzi, a priest of the temple, and he was in training for the priesthood himself when this occured. He became part of the group of Jewish leaders who were forced to march across the desert to a place called Tel-abib.

This forced march caused a crisis among the religious leaders of the Hebrews, who, like the other nations of that time, believed that they could only hear the voice of God in their own land. Many believed that God's power was certain only in the land which God had promised and given them. Ezekiel, however, continued to practice the faith of his fathers and continued to seek the guidance of God.

In the year 593 B.C., while still in exile, Ezekiel remarkably received a powerful vision of God, who was ready to move again among this people who had been so unfaithful. He was called to be a prophet to a depressed people and to an arrogant enemy in the midst of the enemy's land. He was called to speak both to those who would hear and those who would not. He was called to be courageous and to take a clear stand, but he continued to be reluctant.

Finally God instructed Ezekiel to "eat this scroll" (Ezekiel 3:1) written with cries of grief and to find strength and courage in that. He was to find nourishment in the tale of how his ancestors had found freedom from the Egyptians with the power of God and the gift of God's law. Symbolically, Ezekiel was to make the Hebrew story, told in the law, his story. It would be a story of courage moving toward freedom. Ezekiel had to rediscover that he, like Moses, was created in the image of the God of all the world. Now he was called to help save his people just as Moses had been. The word of God given in the scroll and the image of God in which Ezekiel had been created would be the foundation for his remarkable imagination which would produce memorable visions for his people (such as the valley of dry bones and the river of life) as they sought new life with God.

The Scroll of God—
My Script for Life

The Scroll of God

My ministries are _____

_____

_____

_____

My gifts for ministry are _____

_____

_____

_____

Lott Carey: A Private Decision Made Public

Lott Carey, a black man born in 1780 as a slave, made a decision as a free man in 1817 to become the first black American Christian missionary to Africa. In his farewell words upon board the ship for Africa, he reflected on the decision he had made:

> This step is not taken to promote my own fortune, nor am I influenced by any sudden impulse. I have counted the cost and have sacrificed all my worldly possessions to this undertaking. I am prepared to meet imprisonment or even death in carrying out the purpose of my heart. . . . I feel bound to labor for my brothers, perishing as they are in the far distant land of Africa. For their sake and for Christ's sake I am happy in leaving all and venturing all.[1]

[1]J.B. Taylor, *Lives of Virginia Baptist Ministers* (Richmond, Va.: Yale and Wyatt, 1837). p. 405.

Langdon Gilkey and the Essence of the Image[1]

Just prior to World War II a very young American teacher at Yenching University, near Peking, was captured by the Japanese conquerors of China. The Japanese soldiers herded all "foreigners" from that area into an internment camp in Shantung Province. While this was a harsh experience in many ways, this crucial historical moment also became a creative time for the young teacher who kept a careful journal of events and thoughts.

Langdon Gilkey was the young teacher's name, and he found his thoughts turning to God often at the internment camp as he considered the actions of God's human creations. Through this experience the young teacher grew into a theologian (one who ponders about God and God's relationship to the world), and today this American Baptist layman is known as one of the great theologians of the modern world.

During his time in the camp Mr. Gilkey became overwhelmed by the self-concern and self-centeredness of persons in difficult situations. They were missing the true center of their lives which was God. He believed that the only hope for these people to break out of this pattern and find that true center was to rediscover themselves as creatures of God created in the "image of God." He believed that, as creatures of God, we are called to share in the work of creation. We do this by searching out where God is working in each situation, by recognizing the opportunity and creative possibilities in each situation, and by accepting responsibility to recreate the present and future in the providence of God. Gilkey seems to share an "amazedness of spirit" with Roger Williams. As creatures of God in the image of God, we too are called to create.

[1]See Langdon Gilkey, *Shantung Compound* (New York: Harper and Row, 1975) and *Message and Existence: An Introduction to Christian Theology* (New York: Harper and Row, 1980).

Woven for Weaving

We must think of our own lives in two ways when we are Christians. In one sense we are merely single threads in the Great Weaver's design for life—we are shaped and used by God for God's perfect purpose. But in another sense, we are more than threads; we are weavers as well. As those created "in the image of God," we have been woven by the Great Weaver to do some weaving ourselves in our own limited area of the great tapestry of life. So our faith has a certain tension: (1) We are created by God for God's purpose, and yet (2) we are free to choose much of what we will do in our lives. Think about the specifics of your own life.

God shapes my life daily by:

1. _____
2. _____
3. _____
4. _____
5. _____

I give shape to my own life daily by:

1. _____
2. _____
3. _____
4. _____
5. _____

God and I are co-creators in the creation of my life.

Unit II.

THE STORY OF BROKENNESS

The loom upon which the weaver weaves is filled with broken strands of yarn and loose ends. These broken ends are not in sync with the work and plan of the weaver. However, the weaver must work to create the perfect pattern and structure of the tapestry by using these broken threads even in spite of them.

God, too, must continually create and tell the story of life despite the separation all persons experience from God in sin. Our separation from God, the brokenness of all life, is not the end of the story, but it is an inevitable part of your story as well as of the story of all humankind.

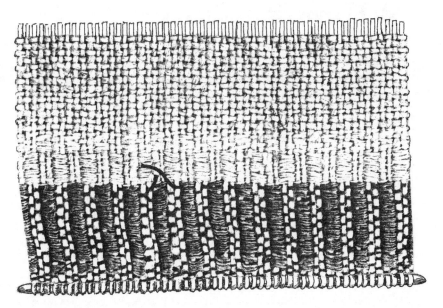

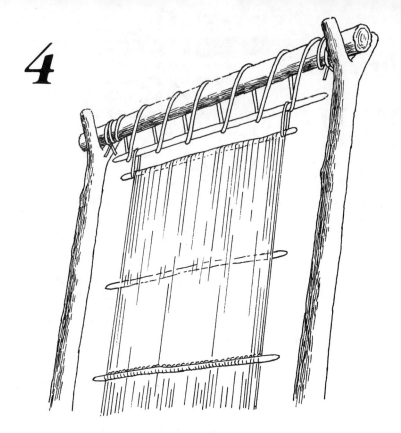

A Loom's Limits

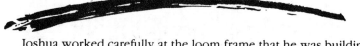

Joshua worked carefully at the loom frame that he was building at home. It was too big to remain in his room but there was a convenient place in the barn, which had once been an office and had heat. It also provided quiet and privacy. He had been comfortable using Mrs. Richard's looms, but she had told him that a real weaver would eventually want to make his own frames and looms.

One day she had instructed him about the construction of looms and frames. She showed him a frame of genuine New Mexico piñon that came from her own mother. Then she showed him one of a dark smooth wood made by a French cabinetmaker which had been a gift from her children. Altogether she kept four frames of varied sizes. She explained why the rough texture of the piñon worked better than the highly polished texture of the other in preventing the yarn from slipping and the fabric from loosening. She taught him how to lash the bottom corners of the frame and how to anchor the frame in place. She also showed him how the y's at the top of the poles must match precisely the diameter of the crossbar.

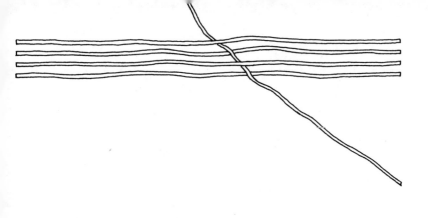

When he had absorbed all these instructions, Joshua had gone out to the woods beyond the west pasture and found his materials. Now the loom was almost complete. He was a little afraid to show it to his teacher just yet. Would it meet her exact standard? Would it be up to the task of enabling him to create the fabrics of which he dreamed? Was it better somehow than that first sorry tapestry he had created, with its ragged weave and crooked edge? When he was finished with the frame and had it anchored in place, he called Mrs. Richards and asked her to come and examine it.

He became anxious while he waited for her to come. The chores were done and he couldn't concentrate on homework, so he swept and cleaned up the old office while he waited. It would take Mrs. Richards a while to walk over. The loom frame was important, she had emphasized; it must be firm without being absolutely taut. That was why metal would never replace wood for the genuine weaver; the little bit of "give" in the natural materials was a gift to the weaving process in the creation of a fine fabric.

Joshua's mind moved naturally to the ways and plans to reorganize the old office for weaving. The pastor had told Joshua's discipleship class that God put a framework into place in creation, a framework to structure the relationship between God and God's people, a framework upon which God could weave the fabric of creation. The pastor had identified this framework as a "covenant." A "covenant," he explained, was like a treaty, an agreement with terms between two parties, a contract which stated the terms of a relationship. In the convenants of the Bible the relationship was between God and God's people. Through these covenants God sought to structure or frame the relationship that was the basis for weaving the fabric of life.

The pastor said that there were at least three of these covenants or frames. The first and most simple was the covenant of creation which is seen in the story of the Garden (Genesis 2 and 3). God created humankind to live naturally with nature, enjoying it and caring for it;

but the man and woman were not to eat the fruit of a particular tree. The framework failed in the episode we know as the Fall. The second covenant was that based upon the promises made to Noah and Abraham, and the tablets given to Moses on the mountain. This is the covenant of law and provides the framework for the stories of the Old Testament. The third or "new covenant" came through God's great gift of grace in Jesus as told in the New Testament, and is sometimes called the covenant of grace or faith or the covenant of love. It is the most flexible and demands a mature, growing relationship between God and God's people. Joshua had never understood how important the frame was before, but his class had helped him to see.

His thoughts were interrupted by a knock at the door. Joshua was startled to see Jessie walk in with her grandmother. Mrs. Richards went right to the frame and began to run her fingers along the edge of the wood. She smiled as she touched the patches of bark he had left on the beams and then she explained to Jessie how important the rough texture was to support the web. She was happy with the warp and web beams. Finally, she said, "The test will be in the weaving. I will want to see how you do both here and on my looms." They set a time for Joshua to come the next day and then they left. Joshua was elated; he was ready to test his loom.

That night he read again from his Bible about the danger of inadequate frameworks. In Jeremiah 31, he read about the change from a covenant written on stone to one written in the hearts of people. In Galatians 3 he read about the old and new covenants again. He remembered the warnings the pastor had given. He remembered the story of Hosea, how he remained loving to Gomer even when she was unfaithful. He remembered the story of an Indian woman named Kim Mammedaty and how she was working to distinguish true and false frameworks for weaving. He drifted off to sleep wondering if he had found the right frame for weaving a life.

Kim Mammedaty[1]

The story of brokenness has always been a real one for the Reverend Kim Mammedaty, the first seminary-trained Native American woman to be ordained by American Baptist Churches, USA. Among her earliest memories are those of people she knew, her people, destroying their lives with alcohol. They were weaving their lives on the inadequate frames of a destructive society, rather than on those of the dignity of the full human relationship with God.

This young Indian woman, too, came to experience the limits of those looms upon which society offers people the opportunity to weave meaningful lives. Following her encounter with Ioleta McElhaney, a Kiowa who came to her church to preach and tell stories and who became a kind of mentor to her, Ms. Mammedaty began to think about ministry. When she discovered limits to ordination that said only male or white persons need apply, she began to understand that the looms that our society provides may not be the looms upon which God will weave our lives. Brokenness became a personal experience.

She began to work at replacing the structures which society offered for weaving her life with the structures of God's grace as she made her way through Eastern College and Colgate Rochester Divinity School. She also began to envision a halfway house ministry for Indian women (which eventually came into being as Hobart House) to enable them to re-covenant with God. The Reverend Kim Mammedaty has continued to be aware of the mixed bane and blessing of the frameworks of existence as she has ministered in the name of Christ and the covenant of new life.

[1]Based on material by Janice Rounds in *Wise Women Bearing Gifts,* Suzan Johnson ed., (Valley Forge: Judson Press, 1988), pp. 43-48.

The Prophet Hosea

Hosea is one of the great prophets of the covenant in the Old Testament, and his story is one of the most daring in the entire Bible. Hosea's story not only reflects on the activity of God in human history, but it also reveals the heart of God as the root of this activity.

Hosea knows the elements of the "legal covenant" between God and God's people in creation very well. He knows its terms, mutual obligations, and value. He compares God's relationship with creation to that of a marriage relationship. A happy marriage has certain characteristics and requires sincere commitment from both partners. But as Hosea looks around him, he does not see the characteristics of a happy marriage in the relationship between God and God's people. He sees instead a broken marriage revealed in the confusion and aimlessness of the people, in the unwillingness of the people to be obedient, and in the lack of justice and caring in the land. He traces the roots of this brokenness to the faithlessness of the people, to their failure to uphold their part in the covenant with God. God, Hosea insists, remains faithful even when the people of God's creation do not.

Hosea had a sudden insight into the heart of God when he examined the materials of his own life. He proposed his own life to the people as a living parable of God's eternal grace. It was a daring strategy. Hosea had married a woman named Gomer with whom he had had three children, but she was not a trustworthy woman and she was unfaithful to the marriage covenant. Their marriage was broken and they were separated. But Hosea did not finally desert Gomer; he welcomed her back into his home to work at the covenant again. God's love is like that, he said. There is a deep longing in God's heart to restore the broken relationship and to effect reunion between God and creation.

This insight in Hosea into God's loving heart sets the foundation for God's new covenant with creation in Jesus Christ. It is a crucial revelation in the unfolding story of the Great Weaver.

Jethro, A Model Mentor

As the deliverer of God's law to his people, Moses became a mentor to his whole nation. And yet he, too, needed a mentor, a guide, a friend. If Moses himself could speak about Jethro, he might say something like this:

"Jethro was such an important person in my life. I guess I should tell you about him, starting at the beginning of our relationship.

"After I killed the Egyptian guard, I was terrified and had no place to go; somehow I decided to hide in the land of Midian. It was there that I met Jethro, a priest of his people. I was a stranger and yet he welcomed me, befriended me, employed me to work with his sheep, and eventually took me into his home when I married his daughter, Zipporah.

"Jethro was a wise counselor who knew that I was troubled and needed to reflect on my life and my God. The training as herdsman that I received from him made me a better shepherd later for my people as we traveled in the wilderness and desert of Sinai.

"When I received my call at the burning bush, Jethro again proved to be a supportive person and told me to return to my people 'in peace.' Even though our religious traditions were different, my respect for him did not decrease with the years. And so it was, when he came to me in the wilderness, that I looked to him again for wisdom and advice, even as my people looked to me. I was pleased to see him; I knew from past experience that he was someone with whom I could share the load of the demands of the people who were becoming an increasingly unruly flock.

"When Jethro watched me work with the people and their concerns, he knew instinctively that the way I was doing it—all by myself—was wrong. The job was too heavy for me; I needed help. I was hoping that he might stay, but instead he showed me a way to organize people, in smaller groups with intermediate leaders and judges, that would make the load easier on me. He helped me to learn to trust others and let them share in dispensing some parts of the law. In so doing, I would have time to be more faithful to God myself. [The story of this change is in the book of Exodus, chapter 18.] Because I trusted Jethro, he could enable me to be a more effective servant of God with my people. Again I found his advice helpful and supportive. I missed him greatly when he left and returned to his own country."

31

Name the Looms

There are many structures, both personal and social, that exist to provide a framework for our lives. Examine the structures that give shape to your life every day. Specifically name each one.

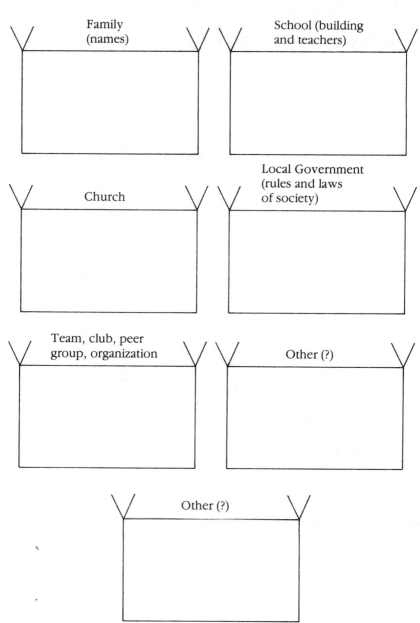

Family
(names)

School (building
and teachers)

Church

Local Government
(rules and laws
of society)

Team, club, peer
group, organization

Other (?)

Other (?)

Bits and Pieces

As Joshua made his way around the barnyard, his thoughts were teeming. His steps were all carefully measured out so that he could rise at 4:45 A.M., complete his chores, and be ready for the school bus at 6:51 A.M. The pens had to be cleaned, his stock fed, and his cows milked before he had his own shower and breakfast. If he stayed on schedule he would be ready six minutes before the bus arrived— plenty of time. Most mornings he made it, but sometimes George had to drive him to school, and more often George or Ella had to pitch in to help him with the chores so that he could get to the bus on time. The timing of his morning pattern was so close that even one small thing going wrong would put Joshua in a bind.

The covenant by which he carried out his morning obligations in this small world of the farm was possible, but often the weather, animals, or equipment had other plans. A sick animal, contaminated food, a hole kicked in the stall, a gummed-up generator could all cost valuable minutes. "Life is what happens when you've made other plans," George was often heard to say. This morning, as Josh realized that he was going to be late yet again, he found himself wondering about the distance between God's plan for life and the way it all really happened. "Brokenness" the pastor had called it, and some days that seemed like a very mild word.

With George and Ella's help, he made it to the bus on time but, as he stretched back in his seat to relax a minute, the word came rushing into his consciousness again—"brokenness." He was surrounded by it. Eric, who sat two seats in front of him on the bus, had recently told him that his parents were getting a divorce. Mrs. Davis, who drove the bus, had lost her youngest son to a skateboarding accident with a hit-and-run driver. The big rumor at school was that Mr. Barkley, the principal, was dying from cancer.

The world was filled with tragedy but there was more. If some people felt separated from God by the circumstances of their lives, others were willfully separated. There was Jake Roman and his roving band of thugs who made life miserable for a wide array of people each day, and there was Mindy Foster who had gotten Josh into a lot of trouble by copying off his last pop quiz in English class. There were so many people who lived as if God were just not there.

And here we are all together on this bus, Josh thought, *all together the ragtag bits and pieces of a broken world, the tangled yarn of a fabric that has ceased to be woven by God's loving hand for some reason.*

"Sin," the pastor had called it. "It's the condition of being separated from God, of living outside of God's covenant, of living in a world no longer adequately structured by God's covenant." When the pastor had first talked about living in sin, Josh could think only of people killing and stealing from others, but the pastor had helped him to see a much bigger picture. Now he was seeing brokenness and sin everywhere. Somehow it went back to God's covenant with creation. When the structure of God's relationship with people was soundly in place there was a wholeness and goodness about life. When that structure was ignored or broken by the creation, the trouble rippled out in every direction both into society and its institutions and into individual lives until it filled everything and everyone.

The noisy bus arrived and the stampede for the lockers began. A new day among the tangles of God's tapestry was here. *Is there something I'm not seeing?* Josh thought. *Is there a hopeful word from the Lord?*

As Josh entered the warmth of Mrs. Richards' entryway that afternoon, he was happy to see Jessie. It was like another world to come here after school; it was like he was reestablishing a connection with something that he had lost once. Was it God's covenant or structure? Perhaps not, but as the writer of Genesis said, "It was good." This house was one part of the fabric of his life where the yarn was not loose and tangled. The pastor had been happy when Josh had chosen Mrs. Richards to be his mentor for the discipleship class and had been amazed to discover his interest in weaving.

Josh noted now that there were now three looms set up around the living room. One was larger than the other. "Before we weave today, I want to show you something," Mrs. Richards was saying. She took down Josh's first weaving from the hallway wall and began to talk about its weave.

"A weaving really isn't judged by its colors and pattern; those come from the personal taste of the weaver. The weaver knows what he or she likes. But it is judged on craftsmanship and skill. The first test of the weaving is its straightness. It should lie flat and its edge should be even. This tells you how well the weaver followed the structure of the loom. If the edge is good, the whole web is probably good."

Josh knew what would happen even before she laid the weaving on the floor by the wall. He had wandered considerably from the straight, firm loom frame.

"A weaving is also judged by its evenness." She held the weaving by the light and rubbed it between her thumb and forefinger. "There are diagonal rows of small holes in any weaving. These must be in a straight line. If they are not [the light revealed to Joshua that they were not], it may be the fault of the working pattern of the weaver or the quality of the yarn that has been spun. That's why careful weavers spin their own yarn. The yarns must match the tools of the weaver. Now let's get to work."

As they began, Joshua considered the difficulties faced by the Great Weaver who must work with yarn that has a mind of its own.

Prophet's Crossword Puzzle

Down

1. I was called as a youth to prophesy to my people.
2. I confronted King David about his treatment of a soldier.
3. I described the suffering servant in words that later described Jesus.
4. I was to be a meal fit for the king of beasts.
5. I was a sheep farmer who came to preach on behalf of the poor.

Across

6. I saw visions and spoke with an angel of the Lord.
7. Some people believe I described a flying saucer in the first chapter of my book.
8. "To do justice, and to love kindness, and to walk humbly with your God" are my most famous words.
9. My famous battles with the prophets of Baal form an important part of the Old Testament.
10. I learned about God's love through my relationship with my wife.

These Scripture references will help you to find the answers:

2 Samuel 12:1-12
1 Kings 18–19
Isaiah 53:2-12
Jeremiah 1:4-6
Ezekiel 1:4-28

Daniel 6:11-17
Hosea 1:2–3:1
Amos 1:1;2:6-8
Micah 6:8
Zechariah 1:9

36   Answers to Prophet's Crossword Puzzle on page 94.

Balthasar Hubmaier and the Protestant Reformation

Balthasar Hubmaier must have had doubts about his own faith on March 10, 1528, when he was publicly burned at the stake in Vienna after several months of imprisonment and torture. But who was this man and why was he killed?

Balthasar Hubmaier was a Baptist and one of the most important leaders of what is called the "Radical Reformation." He was born in the same generation as Martin Luther (between 1480 and 1485), and like Luther, he became a Roman Catholic priest and a seminary professor. As he grew in his relationship with God and studied his Bible, he, too, discovered a different vision of the gospel from that of the church. He became involved in the church reform movement in the town of Waldshut, Germany, in 1524. But he soon had a disagreement with Luther and some of the other reformers. He became convinced of the truth of "believer's baptism" and was rebaptized in 1525.

There were really two Reformation movements in Europe during the sixteenth century. That was a time of great upheaval, anxiety, creativity, and change for the Christian church. We know the names of Martin Luther and John Calvin today from our history books; they were very influential churchmen. These Reformation leaders established strong churches and wrote books of theology. They were able to bring together large numbers of people because they had strong political and military backing and their lives were secure. Theirs is now called the "Magisterial Reformation."

There was, however, a second drama being played out on the stage of sixteenth-century Europe, a lesser-known but no less important drama that we refer to as the "Radical Reformation." In many ways it was a forerunner of the "free church" movement in America and was composed of people referred to as Anabaptists, people like Balthasar Hubmaier. The Radical Reformation was as large as the Magisterial, but its followers had no political protection. Many of its leaders were drowned, burned at the stake, or beheaded before they reached the age of thirty-five.

People like Hubmaier had no time in which to develop theologies, but they did build strong churches based on the New Testament model. Such churches were able to withstand brutal persecution. The radical reformers spoke God's word to all people, whether they heard or refused to hear. The Anabaptists proved again what the first- and second-century churches had learned so well (through the death of martyrs such as Stephen [Acts 22:20]), that the "blood of the martyrs is the seed of the church."

After Balthasar Hubmaier was rebaptized in 1525, he became the primary leader and theologian of the reform movement in the town of Nikolsburg. He was captured, imprisoned, and killed shortly afterward. He is now known as an Anabaptist martyr and is remembered in the Humbaier Memorial Baptist Church in Waldshut, Germany.

Among the theological writings of Balthasar Hubmaier was the first Baptist cathechism or manual of instruction. He was a brave man, unafraid of speaking the word of God as he understood it. He was a unique person whose ideas have enriched our free church tradition today. His gift was courage; he is a model for us all.

John of Patmos

When we talk about biblical writers who were clearly aware of the broken relationship between God and God's creation, John of Patmos stands high on the list. From his writings in the book of Revelation, the final book of the New Testament, we learn that this particular John was a faithful Christian who had been exiled by Roman authorities to the prison island of Patmos near Ephesus. He was probably exiled there during a period of persecution for Christians who refused to participate in the rituals of emperor worship.

John saw little evidence of God's covenant with creation by the time he wrote. The covenant had been smashed. The Divine Weaver had been replaced. The corrupt powers of this world were in control. Governments killed and imprisoned Christians, religious and political cults mocked God, the structures of authority were a confused tangled mass, and the spiritual hopes of people were hanging by a single thread. As he viewed the ugly tapestry of his time, John cried out for a word from God. To state his own hope of a renewed covenant and relationship with God, John adopted the radical approach of apocalyptic literature. Although the Weaver's work had been rejected, John affirmed that God would come again in the person of Jesus to continue weaving this world. It was a promise John drew from his faith in the love and power of God.

In the midst of his despair over a world radically separated from God, the prisoner John experienced a series of visions. He tells us that these visions were given to him by Jesus Christ. They take the form of letters of instruction to the churches of Asia Minor and then an elaborate symbolic allegory of how God will personally reinstate his broken covenant by overcoming the powers of this world and establishing a new Jerusalem, a new heaven, and a new earth. In his vision, John sees God gathering up the fragments of a broken world and making it all whole again. Out of the depths of brokenness and despair, John discovers a new hope for wholeness and a renewed covenant.

When no one else seemed to be listening, John of Patmos, like Hosea, heard again the voice of God reaffirming the love in God's heart for the divine pattern of weaving in the world.

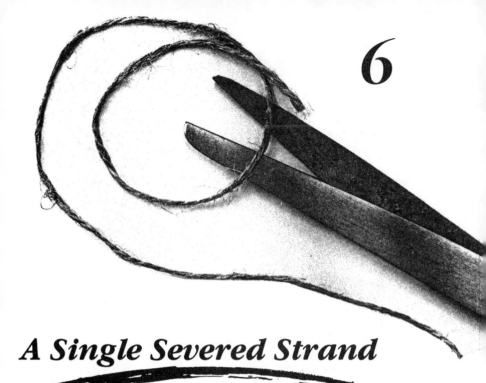

6

A Single Severed Strand

All of this heavy-duty thinking about brokenness had set Joshua to thinking about his own life again. Brokenness was not only something he saw when he looked around at the world but it was something he saw, and more importantly felt, when he looked within. It was a feeling that he could never quite throw off. It was a feeling of discomfort, of not fitting, of separation from something or someone.

His thoughts were moving this way as he continued his work on the new fabric he was weaving. Suddenly Mrs. Richards touched his elbow and told him not to use the strand of yarn he had picked. She told him to put it aside and she would tell him how to use it later. Jessie was smirking from her loom. Josh scratched his head; the yarn looked okay. The color was fine and it was a nice long strand. But he put it aside still wondering what was wrong with it. Usually she explained, but this time Mrs. Richards seemed anxious to get to Jessie and then back to her own loom.

"Maybe it's the color," he said without much conviction toward where Jessie was weaving. But she didn't answer either. She was suddenly very involved in her own work. Well, Mrs. Richards was the expert on yarn. He hadn't learned yet to make and dye his own.

Mrs. Richards told Jessie to walk Josh home at suppertime and since there was no way to get around this direct suggestion, she said she would if he would show her the new construction site first. It was so close that she was sure he knew all about it. He agreed and they were on their way.

The construction workers had all left now, and walking among the partially completed dwellings brought an eerie feeling, like being in a ghost town. But the ghosts here were all of things to come rather than things past. Josh and Jessie were careful not to step on discarded nails and splintered scraps of lumber. They walked all the way through one partially completed structure tentatively naming the rooms and speculating about what kind of family might live there one day. What would the structure be like when it was completed?

Josh grew pensive as they started down the road toward the old farmhouse and so he grew quiet, too.

"I guess the farms around here will all be gone soon," Jessie said. "Suburbs are coming." When Josh didn't answer, she tried a more direct approach. "Are you always so quiet or is it just with the present company?"

"Oh, I'm sorry," he replied, "I've just been doing a lot of thinking lately."

"So have I; let's think out loud together. You first!"

Josh smiled at her enthusiasm. "Do you remember that thread, the one your grandmother told me to put aside?"

"Yes."

"I guess I've been feeling a lot like that single thread lately—put aside, not a part of the big fabric of life."

"But she said to put it aside and save it. Maybe it's special and she has a special use for it."

"No, I think its defective somehow, like she didn't want to use it."

"Tell me more!" she encouraged him.

"We've been having a church membership class at church and talking a lot about brokenness and separation. When I saw that single separated thread, it struck me that I am separated, too. I have this feeling of not fitting somehow. Of course, separation isn't a new feeling for me. I was separated from my mother when I was born and I never knew her. I was separated from many foster homes; some were Navajo and some weren't. When George and Ella finally adopted me, I was happy but I felt separated from my own people. It got worse when we left New Mexico and moved up here. That's why your grandmother was so important—and the weaving lessons. George and Ella encouraged me; they knew it would bring me closer to my roots. Of course the church is so important to them, they're hoping that I will find my spiritual roots connected to God there. That seems possible sometimes in this class."

"When somebody turns you on, you run for a while, don't you?"

Josh smiled at her way of talking. "I guess I do," he said.

"You know, I've been in membership class, too," she said. "I felt like I needed some new friends and a new direction, but my parents didn't seem to care much one way or the other. That's why I came out here. I know my grandmother cares a lot about her church. I've got to make a decision about baptism and I hoped she could help. Our study book is called *Storyweaving* and I kept thinking about her and her weaving. I guess that's why I decided to try my hand at weaving again; the class renewed my interest. You know, I've felt a real closeness to something in all this and I think it's God, but I want to be sure. There sure is lot that gets in the way. Our pastor says that the separation we feel is sin and that everything that we put in the way of our relationship with God or that we let get in the way is a sin.''

"You don't do so bad when somebody turns the faucet on either,'' Josh said as they reached the door of his house. "I feel like some of the separation is beginning to melt; can we talk some more tomorrow?''

"Sure, see you then." And she turned and ran toward the sound of the dinner bell.

The Woman at the Well (John 4:1-42)

It had already been a long and difficult day when the woman approached the well to draw water. The fabric her life was weaving had once more become a confusion of yarn and she couldn't seem to get the threads back in order. The story of her life was a tragedy again. She tried to sort out the threads as she walked but the tangles just got worse.

There were the husbands, five of them, and the latest marriage didn't seem to be any more successful than the others. There were the children, too many of them, tugging at her attention, and the neighbors whose tongues never stopped wagging. Then there was that burning sensation in the pit of her stomach that just never went away. The water from Jacob's well could never quench it. She was not a very happy person. She felt disconnected or separated from something important but she didn't quite know what it was or how to bridge the gap. She was thirsty for something more than water.

She was surprised to see the Jewish man sitting by the well as she approached. It was, after all, a Samaritan well and the Jews had no dealings with the Samaritans. She was more surprised yet when he spoke to her and asked for a drink. Proper men did not address women who were alone in public. She made it clear to him that she was a woman of Samaria and thought that that would end the discussion, but then he said something to her about "living water" and she could not resist following up the comment. Perhaps this was the very man who could satisfy this spiritual thirst raging in her heart. She loved talking theology and so they continued.

Before it was over Jesus had revealed to her his knowledge of her private hurt, her five husbands, and her desire to worship genuinely in spirit and in truth. He finally revealed that he was the Messiah for whom she had thirsted. How he knew her so well she did not know

41

but she was soon certain that she had indeed encountered the Messiah. She ran to tell everyone about the man who knew her better than she herself did and who had reintroduced her to God, the man who had begun to heal the deep brokenness in her life.

Samson

Our text from Judges tells another sad story, the story of a man who never got his priorities straight or lived up to his potential—the story of Samson.

He was the world's strongest man and his feats of strength were very impressive. We might remember how he killed a lion with his bare hands or how he slew a thousand Philistines with the jawbone of an ass. But he is frequently treated like a cartoon superhero and we don't often think about what Samson, the man, was like. We don't often wonder why, with all his strength, he was the only one of the judges who was unable to free his people from their enemies during his lifetime.

Samson, the man, stands in the line of people we know as "judges." These judges ruled Israel between the time of Joshua and the time that Saul became the first king of the Hebrew people. Gideon, Deborah, and Samuel were other famous judges. The judges functioned more like selected tribal chiefs than kings, but none had a story as tragic as Samson. None of them labored under such great expectations as he, and none failed so tragically to fulfill the expectations.

From his very birth, much was expected of Samson. His birth was announced to a barren woman by an angel, who promised that the baby would be a "deliverer" for his people. There are clear parallels here to the births of Isaac and Jesus.

Samson took special vows as a Nazirite, and these vows included not cutting his hair. But his strength was not in his hair; it was in the keeping of his vows. He grew strong in body but not in wisdom. He spent more time getting revenge for tragedies growing out of his relationship with his wife and with Delilah than he spent redeeming his people.

The story of his defeat by Delilah, after three unsuccessful attempts, reads like a TV serial. He was defeated, not by the strength of the enemy, but his own lack of self-control. His promise as a person was unfulfilled because he could not control his temper, his passion, himself. The story of Samson is the story of a man of great gifts and potential who missed the mark, who "blew it."

Even in the end, when he pulled the great hall down on the Philistines, Samson seemed to be motivated by personal revenge. His prayer to God to give him strength (Judges 16:28) was a cry of desperation and involved his own self-destruction. Even in this final self-destructive act, which would redeem his people, Samson's priority seemed to be himself rather than God.

Jamie
Told by Wendell Brooker

I keep a file with a large brown envelope in it in the back of my filing cabinet. It has traveled with me as I have moved, to three cities now, and I can never come across it or open it without a tremendous sense of sadness and loss. It is my "Jamie" file, and it contains a bundle of pictures and cartoons as well as the brown envelope holding the last cartoon and the only letter I ever received from him. Jamie was a warm friend with many possibilities, but in the end his life was one of unfulfilled promise.

I first met Jamie inside the green walls of the children's unit at the

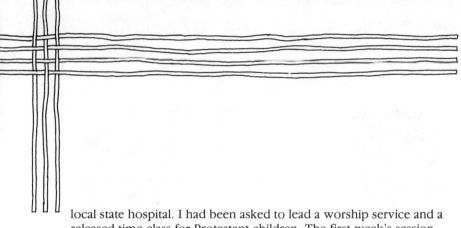

local state hospital. I had been asked to lead a worship service and a released-time class for Protestant children. The first week's session turned into a wild, chaotic experience of screaming, crying, angry foot-shuffling, and confused religious language.

Jamie wandered up to me about halfway through the hour, grinning ear to ear, and gave me some advice in a low voice, which seems to have become gospel for so many law-and-order politicians. I had to ask him to repeat it, but I had heard it right the first time. He suggested that if I brought a gun next time and shot just one kid, I would quickly earn the attention of the rest.

I never brought a gun, but I learned to look forward to my weekly encounters with "the word according to Jamie." He was a long, lean, pale young man who looked even younger than his fourteen years and whose soft voice and quick, sensitive wit demanded hearing. He began to bring pictures and cartoons that he had drawn to the meetings, evidently spurred on by my chuckling over his dry humor and my enthusiasm for his abilities.

After his release, he occasionally appeared at our church youth meetings and one spring went camping with us. When we reached the campsite, Jamie disappeared into the woods while the others made camp. I found him with a baby bird, a wing broken on its first flight. I left him and he sat with the bird for five hours until it died; he buried it and rejoined us, more quiet than usual, at campfire time.

Jamie wandered into and out of our lives for the next few years. He tried special school programs but the only success he ever seemed to have was at the museum of art, where he studied and worked once in a while. Suddenly, one day he announced that he and a friend were going to New York City on motorcycles. He was filled with a new eagerness about something.

His funeral was three weeks later. The impact of his crash had been awesome and there was nothing left to see. The envelope arrived the same day. It contained a letter that said, "I wanted you to have this; you always liked my pictures." The cartoon was of two grotesquely ugly people laughing at each other. He never saw the beauty and potential in himself or in others. Suicide among the young is always a surprise, but it is rarely a mystery. The grief over the loss of Jamie and his potential will always stay with me.

Jacob's Legacy

Jacob might have told his story this way:

"Separated . . .it was something I had felt painfully for years. I was separated from my brother, my people, my God. I had stolen my brother's birthright years ago and had run away to avoid punishment. The physical separation from all I had known only reinforced my spiritual isolation. It was the spiritual pain that hurt so much. While I had saved my life and even prospered in some ways, I had not found peace.

"Finally I could bear it no longer. I had to go home. While it turned out to be more difficult than I thought it would be to leave my new world, my father-in-law's world, I finally outwitted him and paid my obligations in full. I was on my way. Along with my flocks, my wives, my children, my servants, I headed for the river Jabbok and sent word to my brother Esau that I was coming.

"Even though the miles melted away, my inner turmoil would not. Something would not let me rest—fear, anger, and confusion com-

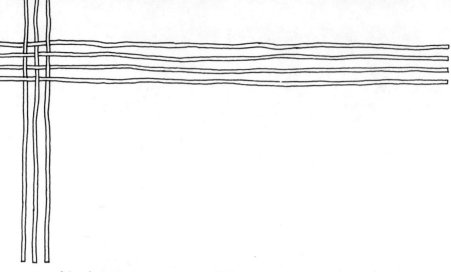

bined to create an anxiety within me that only intensified as we progressed. Finally, the night before we were to meet Esau, I withdrew from the group to sleep alone. I did not want to cause distress for anyone else.

"But as I tried to sleep, someone came to attack me and we wrestled until dawn. First I thought it was a robber, then I thought it was a demon or an angel. Finally I wondered if it was God. Whoever it was, I would not let go until I had received a blessing. The night wrestler touched my thigh and left me with a lifelong crippling wound for a blessing, but suddenly I knew that the physical wound was only a sign of the spiritual wound that I had carried for too long. I had seen God face to face and lived [Genesis 32:30]. I had rediscovered a relationship with God in my nighttime struggle and somehow that renewed relationship strengthened me for the encounters with my brother and my people. The openly acknowledged wound that could now be seen by all paved the way to a new life.

"Isn't it mysterious how in the depths of sin and separation, God comes to us and wounds us with a blessing and brings us home? The pain of brokenness is never the end; it is a beginning."

Baptists have been no strangers to the legacy of separation from people and from God of which Jacob speaks. The Anabaptists of the sixteenth century were outcasts from their society. Bunyan was an outcast in his seventeenth-century society and knew well the inside of a jail. The first Baptists in the New World were cast out from both old and new England. The first "new light" Baptists led by Isaac Backus were cast out of the Puritan Congregational churches. William J. Simmons, who helped form the National Baptist Convention, and Martin Luther King, Jr., who led the civil rights movement of our century, knew the separateness caused by race. All of these must have wondered at some point if they had been separated from God, too. And yet, they persevered and discovered God anew in the legacy of the struggles of their dark nights and wounded lives.

Unit III

THE STORY OF TURNING

Loose and broken strings mar the texture of the uncompleted fabric. An adjustment by the weaver opens the possibility of new connections in the pattern of creation. In order to find its proper place, each loose string must be properly tied by the weaver. The graceful fingers of the weaver will make these knots possible and redeem the pattern. The weaver's comb tamps each joined thread into its proper place. When every loose end is redeemed, the pattern will be perfect.

When people are broken or lost, they seek a God who can mend or redeem their lives. They know that they need to turn toward God in order to find their places in the fabric of creation. Through the sacrificial love of Jesus, signifying the new covenant of God's grace, each person and all people are enabled to make this turn. God provides the necessary forgiving fingers for the persons at loose ends through the ministry of the church. The act of baptism symbolizes the knot or tie that brings the broken person into the divine pattern. The discipline of the new life of discipleship tamps the disciple's life into its proper place in the fabric of creation. The possibility of genuine ministry is born.

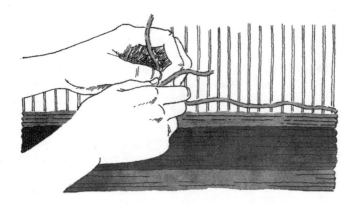

Forgiving Fingers

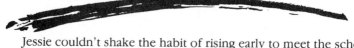

Jessie couldn't shake the habit of rising early to meet the school bus. It was 6:30 A.M. when she quickly made her way to the ponder place on the porch. As she began to rock the chair, she could see the lights down the road, the product of power plants, wires, and bulbs, and imagined Joshua completing his chores. Those lights began to fade as the sun rose, gradually lending its luster to the road, the farm, the countryside, the encroaching houses. She wondered if the chipmunks and rabbits loved the sunshine and warmth as much as she did.

She thought about Joshua and their conversation last evening. Another kind of light was beginning to lend its luster to Jessie through him. He might feel separated from others, or unsure of himself, but she felt drawn to him. He could be a good friend. He had survived a much more difficult life than she, but they were asking the same kind of questions. What was the aloneness she felt ? Who would help her overcome it? Her thoughts about God were crystallizing. When Joshua spoke about the separateness he felt from his people and his heritage, Jessie realized that it had never even occurred to her that she really had a people or a heritage. She had just sort of stumbled through life feeling "lost," but until this baptism class she had not realized "lost from what." She was beginning to see; she was lost from God. She was a broken string—a lost string —in the carpet of creation. God had been working to bring her back into the fabric, but she hadn't yet recognized God's efforts. Was she ready yet to respond?

The sky had moved from black to orange to pink to blue to nearly white as she thought. Joshua's school bus had long gone. She was barely aware of her grandmother who was suddenly at her side with a little tray, two cups of hot chocolate, and some almond cookies.

"You're up early," she said.

"Habit, I guess," Jessie replied. "I can't shake it."

"Habits can be good things," Mrs. Richards remarked. "Tell me what's on your mind."

"Church! No, God, really. I can get baptized in a couple of weeks if I want to."

"Will you want to? Don't do it unless you know, really know down deep, that it's right. God is more than a habit, you know."

"Yes, I know that's right. Church might be a habit, but I do believe God is more than that. I guess I came out here looking for some help. I know how much church means to you."

"It's true, my church means a lot to me. It's a lot more than a habit. But tell me about your church."

"There's not too much to tell, I guess. There's a building and some people who come together to worship or study once or twice a week. We try to help other people. . . ."

"What kind of people are there?"

"All kinds, I guess—men, women, kids, old people, young people, black people, white people, Hispanic people, Hmong people.'

"Isn't that kind of special? What brings them all together? It takes more than an invitation."

"I guess that's what I'm looking for; I'm not quite sure. I feel kind of lost or unconnected to something and I have this feeling that maybe the church has that place or person or life I'm disconnected from. Maybe that's why all those people are there. Maybe they've found something. Our pastor says that our church is special; we're fortunate to be in the city where we can be there for all kinds of people. He told our class about sin and separation from God and how important it is to get reconnected. Maybe that's what it's all about—getting reconnected to God and each other."

"I was watching you this morning while you watched the sunrise," Mrs. Richards said. "You were thinking so hard that I didn't want to interrupt; but sometimes I think of my church as a place where I go with some other folks to see and to feel God's sunrise. It's more than a building, or a group of people, or a mission; it's a place where folks gather to receive the light that God gives. Jesus said 'I am the light of the world.' When we're lost, he's the light that guides us home; when we can't understand, he's the light that shows us the truth; when we are separated, he's the light that will be a focus to bring us together."

"It seems to work that way for you and for some other people, but I keep wondering if it's like that for me," Jessie said. "The pastor told us that Jesus is a redeemer; he is a bridge or path to God."

" 'I am the way,' Jesus says in John," Jessie's grandmother replied.

"It makes sense; I know it with my head. I'm not sure I know it with my heart yet. God is there in Jesus, but is God there for me?"

"That's something only you can know. I can only tell you that I

49

know God is there for me. It takes time and our understanding comes gradually, in stages. Have you noticed that carpet in your room?"

Jessie responded, "Yes, the one with the landscapes. It's like a series of landscapes."

"Not quite. Actually, they are all one landscape seen from different angles. They are a version of the land around my grandfather's home in Arizona as I remember it. The land is too big to capture from one angle, or from seven, but I was trying to show its depth, its variety, its power. It's one of my favorite weavings. God has been weaving the story of creation and of the nature of our relationship for thousands of years. This relationship is too big to capture from one angle, too. We can see in the Bible how it was revealed in different ways to Adam and Eve, to Moses, to the prophets, to the psalmist, and to the church in the New Testament. God has been weaving a great variety of stories, pictures, and metaphors of how we get reconnected because God knows that each of us is created differently, even uniquely. Each one of us might need a little different angle of vision to find the redemption that God offers. Jesus is the Redeemer of the new covenant but the writers of the New Testament give us a variety of pictures, titles, and metaphors through which to understand him. God offers each one of us a way. There is one there that will help you know that Christ is the Redeemer just for you when you find it."

"Do you really think so?"

"Yes, I do," said Mrs. Richards. "The light of the world is the one I like, but you will find one, too. I don't know what's gotten into me; I feel like a professor this morning. Now, come with me. I want to show you something."

They walked together to where Jessie had been weaving the day before. Something was wrong; she could see immediately that the weaving was tilted strangely on the loom. Her grandmother placed her hand under the fabric and showed Jessie where one of the warp strings had broken. "This happens sometimes," her grandmother was saying. "It might have been a bad piece of warp but I think you were just weaving too tightly; there was too much stress on this piece."

"It's ruined, isn't it?" Jessie asked, as if she'd already decided to take it apart strand by strand to begin again.

"No, I want you to watch carefully now."

Jessie watched as her grandmother cut the edges of the broken warp and then cut a new little piece of warp and tied it into the fabric with two tight and perfect square knots. Then she trimmed the edge and kneaded the other threads around with her forgiving fingers until the shape of the fabric was restored and the repair work was covered with weft threads. The wound was healed; it looked like new. Jessie looked at her own fingers. Could they be so skilled and forgiving?

"The next time this happens, you will repair it," her grandmother said. "But for now this new little piece is an integral part of the fabric. It's time to go to work again."

Titles of Jesus

1. "Sir, I perceive that you are a_____." John 4:19
2. "You . . have been brought near in the blood of Christ. For he [Jesus] is our _____." Ephesians 2:13-14
3. ". . . for to you is born this day in the city of David a _____, who is Christ the Lord." Luke 2:11
4. "And the _____ became flesh and dwelt among us." John 1:14
5. "Behold, the _____, who takes away the sin of the world!" John 1:29
6. ". . . but emptied himself, taking the form of a _____." Philippians 2:7
7. "I am the _____ of life." John 6:35
8. "I am the _____ and the _____." John 11:25
9. "I am the true _____." John 15:1
10. "Since then we have a great high _____ who has passed through the heavens, Jesus, the Son of God. . . ." Hebrews 4:14
11. "As he [Jesus] was now drawing near . . . the whole multitude of disciples began to rejoice . . . saying 'Blessed is the _____.' " Luke 19:37-38
12. ". . . Christ Jesus himself being the _____." Ephesians 2:20
13. "I am the _____ of the world." John 9:5
14. " 'I know that _____ is coming' . . . Jesus said to her 'I who speak to you am he.' " John 4:25-26
15. ". . . but the _____ has nowhere to lay his head." Matthew 8:20
16. "And they said to him '_____,' (which means _____), 'where are you staying?' " John 1:38
17. "I am the good _____." John 10:11
18. "I am the _____ of the sheep." John 10:7
19. "I am the _____, and the _____, and the _____." John 14:6
20. "Truly, this was the _____!" Matthew 27:54
21. "Grace to you and peace from God our Father and the _____ Jesus Christ." Romans 1:7

Answer Key—"Titles of Jesus"

1. prophet
2. peace
3. Savior
4. Word
5. Lamb of God
6. servant
7. bread
8. resurrection, life
9. vine
10. priest
11. King
12. cornerstone
13. light
14. Messiah
15. Son of man
16. Rabbi, Teacher
17. shepherd
18. door
19. way, truth, life
20. Son of God
21. Lord

51

Paul

It was light that marked the conversion, the crucial moment of turning, for the most famous of the New Testament apostles.

The light did not come upon the brilliant and zealous young rabbi named Saul of Tarsus like the forgiving fingers of a gentle sunrise. Rather it came like an exploding fireball ripping away his eyesight and splintering his conscience. According to the way Luke tells the story (Acts 9:1-31), the encounter was so overwhelming that it knocked Saul to the ground. This intense encounter with God's light was also an encounter with Jesus Christ as a revelation of God.

So overwhelming was the young rabbi's experience with God through this light that his life was completely turned around. He changed his name from Saul to Paul and gave up persecuting Christians to convert people to Christ. It was a 180-degree turn. The light of Christ and the turn toward God are all wrapped up in one motion for the apostle Paul.

Isaac Backus: Disciple of God's Light

> The Lord God is a sun, and when any soul is brought to behold his glories, then eternal rays of light and love shine down particularly upon him to remove his darkness . . . its rays appear to point as directly to us as if there was not another person in the whole world for it to shine upon.[1]

The eighteenth-century Baptist pastor Isaac Backus was a primary mover in establishing the distinctive tone and style of American Baptist spirituality and discipleship. As a young farmer struggling to discover his own salvation in the traditional Puritan way, he came under the influence of the first great awakening. His own spirit was awakened, and the salvation he had not been able to find in his Congregational church, he found alone one day as he was simply mowing his field.

> I went and sat down in the shade of a tree, where my prayers and tears, my hearing of the word of God and striving for a better heart, with all my other doings, were set before me in such a light that I perceived I could never make myself better . . . while I sat there, I was enabled by divine light to

---

[1]William G. McLaughlin, *Isaac Backus and the American Pietistic Tradition* (Boston: Little, Brown, and Co., 1967).

see the perfect righteousness of Christ and the freeness and riches of His grace, with such clearness, that my soul was drawn forth to trust him for salvation.[2]

The light he experienced caused Backus to join with the "new light" church movement. These "new light" churches were originally Congregational (Puritan) churches whose members experienced a new light from God in the great awakening. Many of these became Baptist churches when the spiritual experience of the people was not accepted by the Puritan church officials. The "new light" experience often went hand in hand with ideas of soul freedom, believer's baptism, and an emphasis on spiritual experience rather than dogma and doctrine. Other "new light" Baptist churches were born.

Isaac Backus became a pastor, a pamphleteer and writer, an encourager of churches and church associations throughout New England, an advocate of strong education for pastors through his work with Brown University, and finally a revered Baptist elder statesman. He not only experienced the light when he turned toward it, but carried the light of God with him wherever he traveled. He wrote the first extensive history of the Baptist churches and people of New England and helped weave and shape a meaning of the word "Baptist" that still speaks to us today.

Andy

Andy French was a senior-high church school teacher. He taught that class in our church for many years, and I'm sure no one else would have. He was (and remains) one of the wonders of God's grace in my life. A little man with a bald head and thick glasses, he sat in the third row from the front on the right-hand side of the church with his sister for as long as I can remember.

Neither he nor his sister were married. The church was their family. He was the man who did the children's sermons most Sundays. He worked as a hospital orderly, a job from which he drew many experiences and stories, and in a wood shop of some kind, but he lived for God.

When I left his class and went to college, he wrote me a personal letter each week for the whole time I was there. He did that for each of his students who went to college or into the military. I know he received few letters in return, but that was not his priority; his priority was God. The presence and love of God became very real for me in a concrete way through those letters during those years. Andy was a tower of strength for me not because of his physical stature but, because of his unfailing faith in God and in me. Is there an "Andy French" in your life, too?

[2]Ibid., p. 14.

8
The Tie That Binds

Throughout the day, as Jessie played the role of weaver with the fabric she was creating, she found herself thinking about the weaving God had been doing with and through her own life. She felt a number of strands of yarn coming together with the strand of her own life into a pattern. But the pattern was much more complex than the one she had sketched out with her grandmother before beginning this project. The threads were coming from many directions—from home, from school, from the pastor, from the others in the discipleship class, from the people at the center where she had done her ministry project, from her mentor, from her grandmother, and now from Joshua. She found herself struggling to see and understand just what form this part of God's tapestry was beginning to show.

Jessie had now arrived at a difficult section of her fabric and she wasn't quite sure how to proceed. She had been working with alternating horizontal stripes of gray and white. Suddenly, the pattern called for a mountain; how would she weave it in? The simple "join" that held the stripes together would not work. The pattern required breaking into these stripes at a steep angle to create the figure of the mountain. She asked her grandmother how to proceed. Mrs. Richards showed her how to create the simplest mountain with two lines inclined forty degrees to a peak, and what she called a "lock" where the colors joined in each row. It took Jessie several false starts while her grandmother watched and helped with her own skilled fingers. Finally, Jessie found a rhythm and a black mountain began to take shape, to be locked into place among the stripes.

Her grandmother came back and congratulated her on her work after a while and Jessie found herself thinking about the encouragement that she had received from her mentor as she made her way toward the mountain of life. She began to tell her grandmother about the warm relationship she and Mrs. Hartley had developed. Jessie told her how surprised she was that she could be friends with an adult, especially a teacher.

"Your new friend sounds like a very special person; I'd like to meet her," her grandmother said.

"Maybe you will if you come to see my baptism," said Jessie, then thinking again, "if I *have* a baptism."

"I think I'd like to meet her now. Why don't you call her up and see if there is any chance she can have dinner with us while you're out here."

Suddenly, Jessie wanted to show Mrs. Hartley this weaving.

"That's a great idea. She's off from school this week, too. I'm going to call right now."

When Joshua came to continue his weaving project after school, he stated amazement over how much Jessie had completed. Although it was only a block of several inches, it looked like more because the pattern was beginning to take shape. He ran his fingers along the little ridges where the locks were formed and he expressed his admiration.

"I've been trying to do these locks for weeks and they still don't come out that well," he said.

Jessie smiled but she knew he was telling a little lie. Her grandmother had shown her how skilled he was in another fabric. Also, Jessie was not blind to the shortcomings in her own fabric.

They worked on their fabrics for about two hours and then she offered to walk him home.

"I've been thinking about what you said yesterday about feeling separated," she began as they walked. "I've been working on a project with some people who must feel that way, too. They're called Hmongs; they come from a country called Laos. Their whole tribe or nationality became Christian many years ago and then, when the government changed, they found they were no longer welcome in their own country. Many of them came to America in family and church groups. They were helped by church and mission groups here, but they came from a very primitive place. They worked to find clusters of apartments and homes near the churches that had helped them. They used the churches for community meals and worship and, when some found jobs, they helped the others. The Hmongs used our church that way; the pastor says that they are part of our church family. I kept thinking about how hard it must be for them to be so far from home and in a strange land. But then I would think how great it was that they were so close to one another and could depend on one another."

"I guess no matter how far from home you are, there's someone else who is farther," Joshua said. "But tell me more about how they helped each other."

"Well, I wanted to know more about them and so the pastor suggested that Mrs. Hartley and I could create a ministry project for me with the Hmongs. We started out by talking to the man who was the community leader. He took me to some of the other families where English is spoken. All the children learned the English language in school. Their homes were almost empty of furniture and they didn't seem to have enough clothes, but food was the biggest need. So many people were living on one paycheck that they needed a cheaper source of good food. Somehow writing a report didn't seem like enough."

"What did you do?" asked Joshua.

"One Saturday my father, Mrs. Hartley, and I drove to Kansas City to the Christian center there. They have several Hmong ministries. Rev. Bob Wallace told us about a youth group that came to the center and built some rabbit hutches with the Hmongs and purchased rabbits for them so that they could begin raising rabbits as a food source. He showed us the hutches and rabbits. It seemed like a silly little project at first and I hated the idea of the rabbits being killed, even if it was for food and clothing. But my father and Mrs. Hartley thought it was a manageable project. She said that she knew a cabinetmaker in the church who could help us build, if I could recruit a team of builders from the youth group. You know what? We did it."

"You mean it works?"

"We're not sure yet," replied Jessie. "But we're almost finished with four hutches and the mission committee at church ordered the rabbits for us."

"I want you to tell me if it works; I like a project that really accomplishes something. I think there's too much talking in the church sometimes and not enough accomplishment or action," said Joshua.

"That's why everyone in our discipleship class had to do a ministry project."

"I was reading in my Bible last night from Matthew 25 where Jesus talks about how we can see him if we want," Joshua said. "He says we meet him whenever we meet someone who is hungry, thirsty, naked, in prison, or sick. Jesus says 'As you did it to one of the least of these..., you did it to me' [Matthew 25:40.] I guess you met Jesus when you met the Hmongs."

"I hadn't thought about it like that, but it seems true now that you mention it. The Hmongs taught me a lot about Jesus in the way they care for one another. Maybe you can meet Jesus, too, and heal the separation you feel by serving God through the church."

"Yes, maybe you're right. Maybe the act of doing something for someone else in Jesus' name will be the bridge or the 'join' or the 'lock' that will finally bring me closer to God."

They both smiled at the metaphor.

Joshua said, "I like your project; maybe you're closer to 'the tie that binds' than you know."

"Talking about locks, can I lock you in for dinner tomorrow? Mrs. Hartley is coming out to meet my grandmother. I'd like her to meet you, too."

After they agreed on a time, Jessie walked back toward the lights at her grandmother's home, where a good meal was waiting.

The Story of Esther

The story of Esther, the Jewish queen of Persia, is one of the least familiar but most intriguing stories of the Old Testament. It is the story of a woman who saved her people from destruction, a woman who was in the right place at the right time.

56

The story took place during a time when many Jews were living in exile in Persia. Esther was a young woman living with her cousin Mordecai, who was a friend or advisor to the king's court. When the king desired a new queen, Mordecai arranged for Esther to be considered. She found favor in the eyes of King Ahasuerus, as he was called. She became his queen.

Soon after that a man named Haman became the chief advisor to the king. He was an arrogant man who wanted everyone to bow down before him. Mordecai refused, probably for religious reasons, and this caused Haman to be angry with him. Haman found out that Mordecai was a Jew and plotted to have all the Jews in the kingdom killed.

Mordecai found out about the plot and told Esther that it was her duty to intercede with the king on behalf of her people. He warned her that as a Jew, even though she was the queen, she was in danger also. He believed that it was her destiny to save her people and asked the question "Who knows whether you have not come to the kingdom for such a time as this?" (Esther 4:14).

Esther managed to get the king's ear, risking the king's favor and her life. She outmanuevered Haman, who ended up being hung from the gallows he had had built for Mordecai. The anti-Semite was defeated, Esther saved her people, and Mordecai was made chief advisor to the king. The whole story is very carefully developed to show how God works in history through the courageous decisions of faithful people.

The Right Time, The Right Person

Rosa Parks was a small black woman who worked as a seamstress. She was a polite, intelligent woman who was tired and whose feet ached after a long day when she got on the Montgomery bus to go home. On that December day in 1955, the bus became crowded with shoppers. When there were no more seats for white passengers, the driver asked several black women in the first two rows of the "Negro" section of the bus to move to the rear of the bus to stand. They all did except for Rosa Parks, who politely said "no." She was tired and cold and sore; she felt she could not move. The driver found a police officer who arrested her.

It was a simple incident, which might have been easily forgotton along with thousands of other racial incidents during those years, but Rosa Parks would not let it go. She was a friend of E.D. Nixon, a local black leader who had been trying to find a test case to challenge the law. He asked her if she had the courage to stand as a test case and perhaps to lose her job and be forced to move to another community. She said she was willing to take a chance for justice. She had found the time for which she had been born.

Later, she sat down front at a rally on her behalf and watched a twenty-five-year-old preacher prepare to speak. None of the more experienced pastors in the community would take on the leadership of the committee that E.D. Nixon had brought together on her behalf. They all knew too well what the cost might be. And when it appeared that no one would speak out and call a bus boycott on her behalf, the mantle of leadership fell to a young man, new in the community and to the ministry, who felt compelled to say, at the urging of his older advisors, "Here I am Lord, send me."

As he prepared to speak, he realized that he might be facing the loss of his job, some time in jail, a lifetime of harassment, or even death. As he spoke, the police cars cruised around the church waiting for the people to spill out into the night. He told the story of Rosa and her action quietly and calmy, but then the words began to build and the excitement of the moment began to take charge, and finally the moment came when he could no longer hold back, when he called for a boycott of the buses and a protest against injustice.

"There comes a time," rang his voice, "when people get tired of being humiliated, tired of being kicked by the brutal feet of oppression." The crowd roared its approval. The deed was done, and Martin Luther King, Jr., found the time for which he had been born. He had found his role as God's spokesman for a whole people.

As we consider the simple action of Rosa Parks and the simple decision of Martin Luther King, Jr., in response to the challenge of E.D. Nixon, we can no longer separate them from the massive movement of civil rights that they inaugurated.

Our verse from Esther asks a question: "Who knows whether you have not come to the kingdom for such a time as this?" Esther, Rosa Parks, and Martin Luther King, Jr., saw the time of need with their people. They chose to seize the time.

Risks

Rosa Parks, Martin Luther King, Jr., and Queen Esther risked their lives on behalf of freedom for their people. They all made a judgment that God was calling them to take specific action in a specific situation that would do more good for more people than their own individual lives could achieve. Martin Luther King, Jr., was eventually killed because of the commitment he had made in his own life.

Are you ever challenged to act on your commitments? In what way? How did you respond? Were there family members like Mordecai or friends like E.D. Nixon who stood with you and shared your commitment?

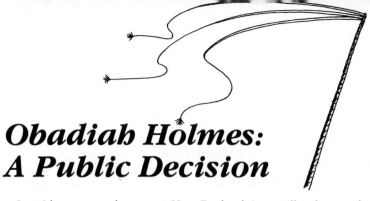

Obadiah Holmes:
A Public Decision

In mid-seventeenth-century New England, it was illegal to teach or preach doctrine or to observe religious practices different from those of the ruling Puritan majority. Believer's baptism fell into the category of unlawful practice. The Newport and Providence areas were being settled by persons who wanted to establish religious freedom for those who practiced such baptism. Among the leaders of the Newport Church at that time was a personally pious and faithful Christian named Obadiah Holmes. In 1651, something happened that caused Obadiah Holmes to make his private faith a public matter; it became clear to him that Christian decision-making takes both public and private forms.

On July 16, 1651 Obadiah Holmes, in the company of John Clarke and John Crandall (also Rhode Island Baptists), made a journey from Newport to Lynn, Massachusetts, to bring Christian fellowship, the elements of Communion, and spiritual encouragement to William Witter. Mr. Witter, who was both blind and advanced in years, had invited them to come to his home for these purposes. During the course of their visit, they found others at his home and the three men from Rhode Island preached the Word, baptized some converts, and served Communion. They were arrested and taken to jail (at the local "alehouse") for their trouble. Finally, after causing a stir at the local church service, they were put in jail in Boston.

After ten days, John Clark and John Crandall had their fines paid and were released, but Obadiah Holmes decided not to accept the offer of payment for his fine and so chose to stand for a public whipping for his faith. He was publicly whipped thirty times with a three-corded whip on his bare back. Just prior to his punishment he said:

> "I am now come to be baptized in afflictions by
> your hands, so that I may have further fellowship
> with my Lord. I am not ashamed of His sufferings,
> for by His stripes am I healed."

When the brutal punishment was finished, he said to the magistrates, "You have struck me as with roses," but for many days he was forced to sleep on his hands and knees because of the condition of his back. Two men who helped Obadiah Holmes stand up after his whipping, John Spur and John Hazel, were jailed and eventually were whipped themselves for showing him compassion. Such was the cost of Obadiah Holmes' private faith becoming public.

Care Word Search

Try to find words that reflect the meaning of being the Good Shepherd.

share, care, carry, time, hands, drive, attitude, self, you, love, garden, tutor, bread (read), befriend, contribute, cash, help, clothes, rake, shovel, smile, feed, energy, lift

S	H	A	R	E	B	R	O	C	A	R	E
C	A	L	O	N	D	S	H	O	V	E	L
A	N	A	G	A	R	D	E	N	E	A	O
R	D	T	L	I	F	T	N	T	M	C	V
R	S	T	S	M	I	L	E	R	A	K	E
Y	O	I	T	B	E	F	R	I	E	N	D
T	U	T	O	R	U	E	G	B	I	O	E
I	E	U	F	E	E	D	Y	U	A	B	E
M	O	D	E	A	C	L	O	T	H	E	S
E	F	E	N	D	A	L	U	E	E	T	L
B	O	R	D	F	S	E	L	F	L	A	B
D	R	I	V	E	H	I	C	K	P	O	N

Answer to Care Word Search on page 95.

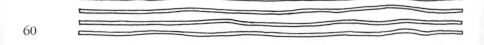

9

A Strand Made Strong

Jessie had never spent a more restless night. The turning toward God that had so intensely gripped her attention this spring now showed itself in the tossing and turning of her sleepless self. Faces, images, and pieces of stories flew through her mind so quickly and piercingly that the relaxation that she normally found in sleep never came.

She imagined herself in conversation with Roger Williams and in a tempest-tossed boat with Lott Carey. Then she was weaving with Esther and Kim Mammadety. But while they weaved, her yarn became tangled with theirs, and suddenly she found herself woven right up into the loom. She saw herself sitting in a field with Isaac Backus, sweating with the heat of an enormous sun, while Martin Luther King, Jr., carried buckets of water down the sunbeams toward her. Her Hmong friends were building houses in the field and she kept seeing Joshua here and there. Jesus, with an inviting smile and outstretched hands, kept walking through all these dreams. At times she felt like a lonely strand of yarn pulled this way and that way. She felt herself being drawn into stories that she could not understand.

It was almost a relief when 6:00 A.M. finally came and Jessie felt that she could get up and escape to the porch into a new day. But there could be no escape from these pictures and stories in her mind until a decision was made. The hot cocoa she made tasted good as she pondered the rising sun yet again.

Jessie and her grandmother worked at their weaving all morning, taking a break at about 10:30 A.M. so that Jessie could learn how to make borders or ridges when they became necessary. These required winding and spinning double- and triple-ply cords on the spindles for such special uses. Her grandmother quoted Ecclesiastes as she began:

> Two are better than one . . . For if they fall, one will lift up his fellow; but woe to him who is alone and has not another to lift him up. . . . And though a man might prevail against one who is alone, two will withstand him. A threefold cord is not quickly broken (4:9ff).

Jessie first watched as her grandmother drew two ends out of two masses of warp yarn on the floor, wound them around her fingers, and then reversed the spindle to retwist the yarn. Again she was amazed at her grandmother's fingers and the strength in the retwisted yarn. Jessie then spent the rest of the morning trying to duplicate what she had seen. Jessie later watched as her grandmother did a triple-ply cord and then doubled two-ply cords into a four-ply cord. But she would not try those until she mastered the two-ply.

Jessie spent most of the afternoon helping to clean the house for dinner guests and then helping to prepare the meal. She marvelled at how her grandmother mixed and matched ingredients, foods, and spices into a story of nutrition that would make this meal a memorable occasion. The mixture of the emerging aromas created a hunger in Jessie. She kept tasting bits and pieces of the meal until her grandmother made her stop.

"It's so much better to taste it all at once," she said, "where every flavor works together with all other others."

Mrs. Hartley was on time and Jessie was glad to note that she and her grandmother found a common bond right away in the identification of the dinner aromas. Jessie temporarily took on the role of mentor as she showed her friend around the house, pointing out its treasures. They freely discussed the weavings in the light of the discipleship class that Jessie was completing.

When Joshua arrived, they took their places at the dining room table and held hands to say grace—an old white grandmother, a black teacher and mentor, a Navaho friend. What a good, strong four-ply cord they made together, Jessie thought.

Mrs. Hartley had several questions about the various fabrics in the house and about the weaving looms she had seen on her brief tour. She shared the focus on weaving from the discipleship class.

"I can see now why it was so important for you to come out here before you made your decision," she said to Jessie. "Have you tied up those loose ends yet?"

Jessie had been aching all day for an opportunity to share her dreams from last night. It seemed like the moment had finally arrived to put things together, to complete at least one phase of the fabric.

She began slowly to describe for the others the turmoil that she had experienced the night before. The sweat began to run as she described the bits and pieces of the dreams she remembered. She lingered a long time on the image of Christ, always beckoning to her as it surfaced in every dream segment she recalled. She couldn't remember how she knew that it was he, but somehow she knew.
" 'Behold, I stand at the door and knock' " (Revelation 3:20), her grandmother quoted as Jessie spoke.

Jessie did not tell Joshua that he had been in the dreams, but she saw him nod when she talked about feeling like a lonely strand of yarn being blown this way and that. The image reflected a moment of indecision he knew well.

Mrs. Hartley responded to the other people in the dreams. "That lonely strand is not as lonely as you think," she said. "There are so many other strands to be tied up with, to be reinforced by. Remember that two- and three-ply cord you showed me? They will make the lonely strand strong as they come together. That's why in our church we have testimonies every week. We need to be reminded that no matter how alone we feel, there is always a great 'cloud of witnesses' [Hebrews 12:1] around us. Giving testimonies was an important part of the African American slave worship. People need to remind one another and be reminded that they are not alone at the crucial moments of life."

"The sea in your dream is the rough sea of life and the sun is the bright light of God," Mrs. Richards said. "And the water must be for baptizing."

"I guess we can tell what's been on your mind," Joshua said. "Everything points toward baptism. Are you going to try it?"

"It's not something just to try," Mrs. Hartley cautioned. "It's something to commit yourself to. I keep thinking of that lonely strand of yarn being drawn and woven into that bigger pattern. You're going to be very uncomfortable if it's not really home to you. You are taking on a whole tradition, taking a place in the big story of the fabric of life that our biblical and Baptists forebears have been weaving for us for centuries. The moment of decision is so important that Jesus told Nicodemus it was like being born again. It marks a great big turn in your life."

"'The creation waits with eager longing' [Romans 8:19] and so do we," Jessie's grandmother said and squeezed her hand.

Joshua was quiet, thinking his own thoughts. Then he simply smiled and nodded his head.

Nourished by the conversation as much as by the meal, Jessie suddenly felt more sure of her place in the fabric of creation than she had ever felt. She felt a smile begin to turn the corners of her mouth; she had never felt so redeemed, so warmed, so lifted by the people around her. It was time to respond to the perpetual invitation of Jesus to a new life.

"I'm ready," she said simply and firmly.

They all knew that she was.

63

Elijah: Seeking the Voice of God

The feeling of fear is often not far from a serious decision. All decisions have consequences. When Elijah became a prophet of God and Ahab and Jezebel became the King and Queen of Israel and slaughtered all the prophets of God with the sword, the consequences of that decision must have been clear to him. Elijah alone was able to escape, first to the desert where God's angel ministered to him, then to a cave in the wilderness where he would be able to hide. He must have felt like a single severed strand of yarn in the story God was weaving.

Elijah, feeling abandoned, was desperate to hear the voice of God. How would God call him? How would God use him as a spokesman against the evil in the land? His was but a single, small voice. He went out to the lip of the cave to feel the wind licking at his face. It was known among the prophets that the voice of God often came with the wind. (In fact the Hebrew word *ruach* might mean either wind or spirit.) But Elijah did not find God there. Where would God be found?

> And behold, the LORD passed by, and a great and strong wind rent the mountains, and broke in pieces the rocks before the LORD, but the LORD was not in the wind; and after the wind an earthquake, but the LORD was not in the earthquake; and after the earthquake a fire, but the LORD was not in the fire; and after the fire a still small voice. And when Elijah heard it, he wrapped his face in his mantle and went out and stood at the entrance of the cave. . . . And the LORD said to him, "Go. . . " (Kings 19:11-15).

The voice of God comes in many shapes and ways. It came to Moses as a fire in a bush; it came to Samuel in an earthquake; it came to Ezekiel in the wind; but it came to Elijah in a still, small voice. Nevertheless, in whatever way it comes, it comes to say, "Go." The voice of God calls people to go and do what is necessary in God's name.

Is God's voice coming to you in some way today? Are you paying attention? Are you being called as a young disciple to "go" and "do"?

Prudence Crandall: A Story of Choosing[1]

My name is Prudence Crandall and I want to share a time of decision in my own life with you. I was a teacher in Canterbury, Connecticut, during the 1830s and after. I was concerned that there were not enough young women being educated in our country, that we were wasting a valuable resource pool, and that too many people were not being fulfilled. After much prayer, thought, and planning, I started a small school for young women in my home. It went well for a few years and, while some people perked up their ears when I told them what I was doing, there was no trouble.

I suppose I was very naive. But when I met Sarah Harris, a young freed black woman who wanted an education, I knew what I would have to do. After spending all night in Bible reading and prayer, I invited her to join the school. This caused more trouble, but she was such an eager student that I finally resolved, with the help of William Lloyd Garrison's newspaper, to invite young black women from all over New England to my school. Seventeen students came the first year.

This did not sit well with the town of Canterbury. We were barred from the Congregational church and unwelcome at the Friends' meeting. I was about to give up on finding a spiritual home for my boarding girls when the Reverend Levi Kneeland of the Baptist Church in Packersville (almost twenty miles away), invited us to worship there.

It was not an easy time. Our well was poisoned with manure, I was forced to endure two long trials, and I went to jail for a while. I would not allow the town to buy up my home and school. My friends in the Baptist church and the wider community, my sister, and my students strengthened and helped me weave the fabric of a courageous story. God always gave me the strength I needed. Mr. Garrison called me a strong disciple.

When Pastor Kneeland's health failed and Rev. Calvin Philleo came from Ithaca, New York, to pastor the church, we found ourselves to be kindred spirits and we married. My school and ministry survived as a witness to the Great Weaver of life.

[1]Adapted from *Prudence Crandall: Woman of Courage* by Elizabeth Yates (New York: E.P. Dutton, 1955).

Santiago Soto-Fontánez: Turning Toward Christ

From the time of his childhood, Santiago Soto Fontánez sensed the work of the Great Weaver's fingers in his life. As a child of the lush, tropical island culture of Puerto Rico, he knew well the wondrous character of creation. But he also became deeply aware, sometimes in personal and painful ways, of the brokenness beneath the island's shimmering surface. A question began to take shape in his mind that gave shape to his living. Whom would he serve with the resources of his life?

Finally pledging himself to serve the Master Weaver, the intense young man prepared himself for his calling with educational degrees from the University of Puerto Rico and the Evangelical Seminary of Puerto Rico. His devotion to his Lord, Jesus Christ, provided him with a model for a serving ministry and the spiritual power to carry it through. He knew down deep that the presence of God all around him and Christ within him required more than an average sacrifice. It required a missionary zeal, the effort to share with others the salvation that had been given to him.

After serving a teaching ministry in Puerto Rico, he moved to New York City to be a pastor. Beginning with a few people, he became God's prime thread for weaving a strong church for those in need of a faith home. During this time he was also earning a Ph.D. at Columbia University and teaching at City University of New York. He was such a strong thread that he was able to strengthen many parts of the fabric of American Baptist Churches.

Dr. Soto-Fontánez became a staff member of American Baptist Churches of Metropolitan New York to direct Hispanic ministries. He counseled with pulpit committees, directed Christian education programs, planned summer camping, and related to the large number of Spanish-speaking youth in the Baptist Youth Fellowship. He also founded the Metropolitan Baptist Institute for training lay leaders.

When American Baptist Educational Ministries needed a strong thread to help develop Christian educational materials for the Hispanic American Baptists, Soto-Fontánez was called. Besides translating materials into Spanish, he produced *Avance,* a national Hispanic newsletter, and *Fe y Vida,* the uniform lessons for youth and adults. These helped weave a national community of faith for Hispanic Baptists.

Dr. Fontánez poured out his life to share the tie that bound him to the Creator and to share the Lord who empowered him, with as many people as he could reach.

Unit IV

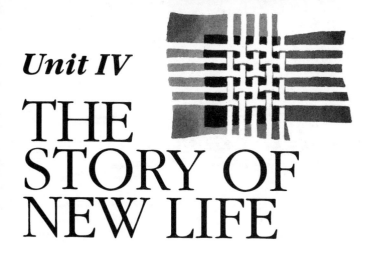

THE STORY OF NEW LIFE

Emerging from the weaver's careful work is a new pattern of a symbol and a story dramatizing God's gracious gift of new life. The growing piece of perfected fabric bears witness to the sustaining craft of the weaver as well as to the renewed strength of the strands of yarn.

Emerging from God's redeeming work of grace is the disciple, a renewed person who will in turn renew the church. With the help and sustaining presence of the Holy Spirit, the disciple is ready to work together with God in weaving the reign of God into the fabric of creation.

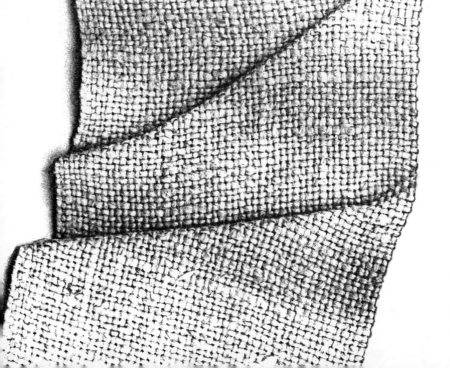

10

The Spirit Thread

Joshua was glad for Jessie. It all made sense to her and that was good. She had thought hard; she had made a decision for new life; she had made a commitment to Jesus Christ. Now she would be baptized and, although there would be much to struggle through, she would be a good disciple. He knew it. He kicked a stone firmly across the ditch that ran alongside the road to Mrs. Richard's house.

It had been an exciting moment at dinner last evening when Jessie had shared her decision. Joshua had felt a kind of electricity in the air when Mrs. Hartley had encouraged them all to join hands around the table to share in prayer. But when the moment passed it had only made the ache in his soul more pronounced. She had committed, but he could not. He had thought about it all the way home last night and now here he was pondering it all the way back. He kicked hard at a lonely stone but the glancing blow only sent it skittering into the ditch. Maybe the problem was that he was giving it too much "thought." What did he sense from God? How did he feel?

Joshua had been taught well in school. His teachers, his pastor, his stepfolks all marvelled at his talent for careful reasoning. But something was not right with him. Joshua wondered . . . Was he the only one for whom careful reasoning was not enough? Faith must be more than the right responses to a few questions. But how was it more? Was he missing something in Jessie's turning experience? Joshua liked the Christian story; the emphasis on creation, brokenness, turning, and new life worked for him, although he felt these more as four pieces of a puzzle to be fit together than as a neat progression. Why then did he still avoid making his own decision? He did not really doubt any of the words of his pastor, but still he hesitated.

Joshua thought about the dreams Jessie had shared. He thought about her single slender thread being drawn clearly into the Christian pattern by the other weavers of the Baptist tradition. He just didn't feel "drawn in" yet. His thread was still flapping loose from God's pattern. What he knew had not yet meshed with what he sensed and felt.

He thought about those words from the apostle Paul—"It is no longer I who live, but Christ who lives in me" (Galatians 2:20). Somehow he didn't yet feel filled by Christ or charged with his Spirit. The ache was still there.

As he worked at the loom with Mrs. Richards, Joshua let his questions and concerns slip out in quiet conversation.

"Knowing is more than with the head; it is with the heart, too, and the spirit," she replied. "Let me show you something."

Mrs. Richards guided him into her living room and told him to look carefully at one of her classical Navaho wall hangings. "What do you see?" she asked.

Joshua described, in some detail, the pattern, the colors, and the effect they created.

"Describe the quality of work," she instructed. He reached up to take the corner of the fabric between his thumb and forefinger and described the fine work in the piece.

"Is there anything wrong?" she asked.

He thought for a moment and then hesitantly answered, "No."

"Look again," she commanded.

"Do you mean a mistake?" he inquired. "I just saw a mistake; I'd never seen it before. Right here there's a little gray thread running through this red stripe. It's only one thread and it's almost completely lost among all the red ones. It's not noticeable at all. I wouldn't have found it if you hadn't pushed me."

"Good, your eyes do see," she replied enthusiastically. "This thread is not a mistake; it reveals a Navajo secret. Perfection smothers the spirit. Every Navajo weaving must have one tiny imperfection, one thread misplaced, or mistied perhaps, so that the weaver's spirit or other creative spirits will not be trapped in the perfection of the rug or fabric forever. It is called the "spirit thread" and it points out from this weaving on to the next, perhaps to a better fabric."

Something clicked for Joshua. "Perfection smothers the spirit." His mind and heart were racing to make connections as he walked back to his loom. Mrs. Richards asked him to retrieve the thread that she had separated out from his yarn the other day.

"This is a good strong thread for your spirit thread," she said. "Weave it carefully in among the others."

He felt a spirit stirring within him, churning and trying to push its way out. Finally he said, "Maybe that's what's been bothering me. The story and the doctrines are all so perfect, but life isn't quite like that. The story of life is never really finished, so it's never quite perfect. But there's a spirit running through our lives, a spirit thread in our patterns, pointing on to the next story. I need to get in touch with that thread; it's that one that gives the new life."

"'The written code kills, but the Spirit brings life,'" Mrs. Richards quoted (2 Corinthians 3:6). "Knowing God, finding new life always involves more than simple understanding. It involves bringing the whole life together—mind, body, and soul, knowing and experiencing—with God's spirit to move into a new story, a new life. I think you are selling Jessie short. Her experience of turning or converting involved so much more than just knowing the facts and deciding with the head. There is kind of a different way that Navajos like to come upon the truth, but this intuitive way to connect with the Creator is not so different as we sometimes imagine. Jesus is still the way. Ask Jessie about it."

Such big thoughts made Joshua's head throb the rest of the afternoon.

After supper that evening, Joshua and Jessie met out by the barn to walk to the place where Joshua had found the wood for his loom. There was a favorite spot nearby that he wanted to share with her, a creek at the far edge of the woods that formed one of the boundaries of the farm. When they sat down by the water, Joshua asked Jessie about her decision.

She was anxious to talk about that special moment with someone, too. "It was sudden," she began, "even though it had been coming for a long time. It was like a whole lot of things all coming together at once, surrounding me like a cloud of witnesses. There were the stories from our *Storyweaving* Guidebook that came out so clearly in my dreams and there was this image of Jesus as the bridge to God, and also the Redeemer who made me worthy to cross over.

"And then the weaving stuff from the book kept coming back to me when I looked at my grandmother, because I always think of her when I think of weaving. I felt a cool porch and a warm kitchen, strong fingers and a firm voice, good meals and lots of love and encouragement.

"Encouragement made me think of Mrs. Hartley. I began to see again in my mind so many moments with her. I saw the trip to Kansas City for the mission project, the evenings at the church building, the rabbit hutches, the conversation with the Hmongs, the testimony Mrs. Hartley gave one Sunday at our church about how Christ sent the Comforter into her life just like the Gospel of John says. I remembered the visit to the church where her father is the pastor—the spirit in the choir, the booming in the preacher's voice, the "amens" all around—and I thought about when she shared her own story about her baptism with me. She always said Jesus had a lot of redeeming to do with her, too.

"Then I looked at you and I ached for you and that separation we talked about. But I felt so much so strongly that I just knew that that separation was gone from me. 'For where two or three are gathered in my name, there am I in the midst of them' [Matthew 18:20]. I felt filled with Christ and with God's Holy Spirit."

"It's the Spirit that's the missing thread for me," Joshua said. "Somehow I know that much."

"There's a verse in Romans [8:26] my grandmother quotes. 'The Spirit helps in our weakness . . . the Spirit . . . intercedes for us with sighs too deep for words.' Maybe you've been trying too hard for words."

She touched his hand with hers and they were quiet for what seemed a long while.

The shadows were long when a furry creature, maybe a ground hog, waddled cautiously up to the stream a hundred feet or so away, perhaps aware of the scent of strangers. Finally, it dipped its face into the water, thristy for the life it offered. As he watched, Joshua felt the Spirit of God well up out of the earth and surround him. A sigh too deep for words escaped him and he sensed that his brokenness was past. The Creator, with help from a new friend, was turning him toward new life, a new life in the Spirit.

Ruth: Making a Choice

It was a time for choosing. Three women stood by the road from Moab to Judah weighing their options. Naomi, the mother-in-law, had accompanied her husband from Judah to Moab about ten years before with her two sons. Both the sons had married Moabite women but now all three men were dead. Naomi had decided to return to her own people in Judah to live out her days.

It was a moment of saying goodbye to a beloved mother-in-law and friend for Orpah and Ruth. Naomi encouraged them to return to their own homes where they would be warmly received. Her future in Judah was uncertain. She had been away a long time; she was unsure who remained to help her. They wept; they wanted to go with her; they could not say goodbye. She explained more forcefully the difficulties that faced her.

Finally, Orpah made her decision and left for a new life with her own people. But Ruth "clung" to Naomi and made a different decision, and made it emphatically. The "weave" of their lives was too tight to leave. Her words have become some of the most famous in all the biblical literature.

> "Entreat me not to leave you or to return from following
> you; for where you go I will go, and where you lodge I will
> lodge; your people shall be my people, and your God my
> God; where you die I will die, and there will I be
> buried. . . ." And when Naomi saw that she was determined
> to go with her, she said no more (Ruth 1:16-18).

The choice was made. She had a people, a tradition, a God whom she did not know. Yet Scripture assures us that her choice was the right choice. She chose the home that was right for her spiritually. She later married Boaz, a relative to Naomi, and mothered a family that eventually produced both King David and our Lord Jesus Christ. Her small strong thread played an important role in the story of God's carpet of creation.

Baptist Name Find

Find and circle the names of forty Baptists in this puzzle. The names are found flowing in every direction—top to bottom, bottom to top, left to right, right to left, and diagonally.

```
M  O  R  I  K  A  W  A  B  B  E  C  M  I  C  F
O  N  R  E  L  L  U  F  E  B  L  B  O  A  U  R
T  C  H  U  G  H  E  S  D  E  E  T  O  R  Y  O
F  K  U  K  O  O  B  E  I  J  I  W  R  I  S  S
O  E  B  R  Y  A  N  I  H  O  L  M  E  S  O  T
S  N  M  A  A  C  E  G  O  U  E  K  R  A  L  C
D  B  A  C  K  U  S  R  I  R  J  N  W  O  R  B
I  S  I  A  R  S  E  I  L  N  O  I  J  O  K  T
C  I  E  R  A  U  S  C  H  E  N  B  U  S  C  H
K  O  R  E  H  B  S  E  B  Y  E  B  D  T  R  U
O  B  E  Y  T  U  B  L  O  C  S  Y  S  R  A  R
C  U  S  H  I  N  G  E  Y  A  E  I  O  O  N  M
H  D  G  E  M  Y  P  E  C  K  X  N  N  N  D  A
U  O  O  N  S  A  Z  F  L  E  M  I  N  G  A  N
C  C  O  R  I  N  S  I  M  M  O  N  S  P  L  T
K  K  D  Y  A  K  G  R  E  B  L  H  A  D  L  W
```

An ABC of Baptists

From the following list of Baptists whose lives are interesting and significant story witnesses to faith, which ones can you identify?

Adams, Jennie Clare
Allen, Thomasine
Apolinaris, Yamina
Backus, Isaac
Bethune, Mary McLeod
Broadus, John
Brown, Carrie Bell
Bryan, Andrew
Bunyan, John
Bushyhead, Jesse
Carey, Lott
Carey, William
Chuck, James
Clarke, John
Clough, John
Conwell, Russell
Crandall, Prudence
Crawford, Isabel
Cushing, Ellen Winsor
Dahlberg, Edwin
Denck, Hans

De Reyes, Marilu Dones
Dubois, Rachel
Fleming, Lulu
Fosdick, Harry Emerson
Frost, John
Fuller, Andrew
Gilkey, Langdon
Gong, Dong
Harper, William Rainey
Henry, Carl F.H.
Holmes, Obadiah
Hubmaier, Balthasar
Hughes, Charles Evans
Jones, David
Journeycake, Charles
Judson, Ann and
  Adoniram
King, Martin Luther, Jr.
Knibb, William
Leile, George
Mammedaty, Kim

Mays, Benjamin
Montgomery, Helen
  Barrett
Moore, Joanna
Morikawa, Jitsuo
Oncken, Johann Gerhard
Peck, John Mason
Rauschenbusch, Walter
Rice, Luther
Rivera-Ortiz, Julia Ester
Rockefeller, John D.
Sattler, Michael
Setzkorn, Mary
Simmons, William J.
Small, Sarah
Smith, Samuel
Smyth, John
Strong, Augustus Hopkins
Thurman, Howard
Webb, Mary
Williams, Roger

Answer to Baptist Name Find on page 96.

John Clarke

The doctor slid down to his knees, covered his face, and quietly uttered heartfelt thanks to God. The moment had been twenty-five hard years in the making. The charter that secured civil and religious liberty for the colony of Rhode Island was signed by King Charles II. The date was July 9, 1663. God had been faithful again and Dr. John Clark felt richly confirmed in the task of ministry that his congregation had commissioned him to do.

Memories tumbled through his thoughts as he knelt in prayer. There were memories of how he had been driven from Massachusetts Bay by the Puritans in 1638 for daring to voice positive opinions of believer's baptism, of how he and others had finally purchased land from the Indians in 1639 and named the land Rhode Island, of how he had become pastor of the Newport church in addition to practicing medicine, of how he and John Crandall and Obadiah Holmes had been arrested for sharing Communion with a sick friend in Massachusetts, of how Obadiah had been publically and brutally whipped, and of how he had reported the religious scandal of the New World in his book, *Ill News from New England.*

He remembered, too, how he and Roger Williams had been elected by his friends and followers to travel to England to secure a charter for Rhode Island in 1651 and how Roger Williams, discouraged when Cromwell fell from power, had returned to the New World in 1654. Finally he remembered working and lobbying night and day for the next nine years in order to see this mission completed and religious freedom legally won. And now the day was here. Praise God!

His prayer came in sighs too deep for words as he felt the intercession of the Holy Spirit. What a comforting, sustaining, and empowering presence the Holy Spirit had been for him. He thought about the words of Jesus in John's Gospel as he spoke to his disciples about the coming of the Holy Spirit, "I will not leave you desolate" (John 14:18). Never alone—the promise had been fulfilled with him.

There would be no legal bonds on that Spirit now in the colony of Rhode Island. Public pursuit of the comfort and challenge of the Holy Spirit would be legal for all persons. John Clarke was ready to go home to that glorious established homeland where the code of laws would now clearly state "that none may be accounted a delinquent for doctrine." He would go home a free man, bearing freedom of soul for all the others as well.

Definitions

Redemption

Salvation

Conversion

Baptism (by Immersion)

Church Membership

Discipleship

A Place in the Pattern

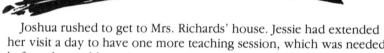

Joshua rushed to get to Mrs. Richards' house. Jessie had extended her visit a day to have one more teaching session, which was needed before she could continue weaving on her own. This session was on some of the preparations for weaving.

"The best weavers," Mrs. Richards began, "always make their own materials for weaving. They not only make their own looms but their own threads, both warp and weft. Some even make their own vegetable dyes. The Navajo dyes are not difficult to make, but some of the materials needed are not available in this part of the country. One day I may be able to show you how to make them, but for to-day we will use some that I have ordered from trusted friends. What's most important to most weavers is the strength, quality, and character of the yarn. That's where we will concentrate today. You must know how to use towcards and a spindle to make your yarn."

Josh and Jessie watched as Mrs. Richards took a small wad of wool and placed it on the sharp teeth of the lower wooden card. She pulled the upper card firmly over the lower so that its teeth pulled through the wool. She repeated this motion several times and once removed the wool to reset it and move the cards in the other direction. She stopped occasionally to take out the little burrs and other foreign objects that did not fall out on their own. Josh noticed that the wool was becoming cleaner. Finally Mrs. Richards had a light, fluffy rectangular pad of wool ready for spinning.

Now it was time for Josh and Jessie to try. The moving back and forth, which made the carding look so easy in the hands of the teacher, was not there for the students right away. Their movements were more jerky and uneven. The result was longer in coming. It took a long time and their wrists got tired before they found a comfortable rhythm. But finally each had a little pad for spinning. Mrs. Richards placed a second wad of wool on each tow card and told them to begin again. She said that they would find it easier now.

When they had each completed carding a third wad of wool, she began to teach them the use of the spindle. They marvelled at the skill in her fingers; they saw no sign of her age. Mrs. Richards showed them how to operate the small spindle and demonstrated why the spinning process must be completed twice for the yarn to be ready for weaving. Even then the yarn often had to be pulled or twisted further to make it ready.

Joshua and Jessie took turns with the spindle. They were each sensitive to the eyes of the other as they went about the task of spinning. The first threads were a disaster; they were very uneven and there were tufts of fuzz which needed to be pulled off the fiber. Joshua and Jessie would both need a lot of practice.

Finally Mrs. Richards showed them how to dye the completed threads of yarn and hang them for drying. This was by far the easiest process of the three.

Mrs. Richards brought out a shopping bag filled with wool prepared for spinning. "Jessie, I want you to practice spinning for a while so I can watch your work. I won't see you again for a while and it is important to get off on the right foot with spinning. Joshua, I want you to do some more carding and keep the bag full. Then when the threads are spun I want you to dye them red."

Mrs. Richards had been thinking hard about Mrs. Hartley's discussion of the *Storyweaving* Guidebook and she could not help reflecting on the analogies between weaving and God's work as she watched and helped her two younger disciples at work. She talked about the care with that God prepared the threads for the tapestry of creation, about the work of the Great Weaver in carding out and cleaning up the raw materials of life, of spinning these out into threads, the twice-born lives that God would use to weave the story of God's reign. She also spoke of the dye into which the yarn was dipped as the tint of a particular tradition, like the Baptist tradition.

Mrs. Richards quoted the apostle, "'The creation waits with eager longing for the revealing of the [children] of God' [Romans 8:19] just like I am waiting for these threads you two are making."

Josh listened intently as she and Jessie talked back and forth. He was beginning to make some connections of his own as he continued to work.

Saturday dawned brightly for Joshua as he rose to complete his chores. Jessie had disappeared toward home with a promise to visit again soon and to write, her new life firmly in tow. The sun warmed him with a promise of new life as well. He had an appointment with the pastor to confirm his own decision for baptism.

The little church building was a bustle of activity when Joshua arrived to knock at the door of the pastor's office. The BYF rummage sale was today and members of the youth group were busy sorting, arranging, and pricing. At the center of the social hall was a carpet from Mrs. Richards that would be sold to the highest bidder and that would help pay for their trip to Green Lake this summer. Joshua would help with the sale after his appointment.

It had been a couple of weeks since they had completed the discussion of turning toward Christ and now the pastor was completing private interviews with each member about his or her decision. The office was comfortable, with just enough clutter to make it feel like home.

When the pastor asked if Joshua had made a decision, he began to share his spiritual experience by the creek with Jessie. It didn't seem like much of an experience as he described it and suddenly he was afraid that it wasn't enough. He felt like apologizing; he felt himself shifting gears. "My story's nothing like Roger Williams or Obadiah Holmes standing up to the Puritan authorities, I guess, or those Anabaptist people who were jailed and killed, or the Judsons or Joanna Moore or the Pecks going out to be missionaries, or Helen Barrett Montgomery and her faith, or Martin Luther King."

"Whoa, hold up!" the pastor said. "You're confusing two things. You are beginning a new life. Each one of those people began a new life at one time, too. Let's look at Hebrews 11 for a moment. This chapter is sometimes called the 'faith hall of fame.' Noah and Abraham and Moses and Gideon and David and prophets like Isaiah did not have lives that seemed so significant before they had their crucial encounter with God and said, 'Here am I, Lord, send me.' Their ministries came later. In our class we can do a 'Baptist hall of fame.' We focus on people who did great things just like the writer of Hebrews, but sometimes we forget that it all started somewhere for them with an experience of the Holy Spirit and God's grace speaking to them and empowering them. They are neither unique towers of strength who cannot be matched nor rummage goods from the past, like all those things out in the hall, that can be discarded. They are spiritual guides who were composed of flesh and blood like your own. There was a simple moment when each of them felt the presence of God and then felt a faith well up within them that said, 'Faith is the assurance of things hoped for, the conviction of things not seen' [Hebrews 11:1]. The moment of empowerment came first; then discipleship followed. And for them, that moment may not have been so different from your simple time by the creek. It's a wonderful moment you've described; don't put it down."

Joshua felt encouraged. "You mean the new life might really be here for me?"

"I believe so," the pastor said. "We've been examining a great cloud of witness from the Bible and from Baptist history in this class, but it sounds to me as if you have had the kind of experience that will let you 'run with perseverance' the race set before you. It's receiving the Spirit that has always been a strong characteristic of the people of God. None of them knew what lay before them when the Spirit came with its challenge, and neither do you. We know they were empowered for a new life. We believe you will be too."

"I was afraid my experience was too different or inadequate," Joshua replied.

"The Holy Spirit works in many mysterious ways. Baptists have always appreciated the variety. There's not any one particular way to experience and serve God. This was a special experience because it was first, but you will have others. Yours seems to be real to me.

"The church exists," the pastor continued, "as the place where people in all their variety come together to share their faith and do ministry and mission that they cannot do alone, and to guard the freedom and value of each individual person. Our denomination exists as a ministry of churches like ours to accomplish those bigger ministries and missions that churches cannot accomplish by themselves. Remember when we talked about soul freedom? One of the denomination's large tasks is to model and protect the soul freedom of Baptist people and the autonomy of its free churches.

"You were talking about weaving with your mentor a little while ago. God needs strong disciple threads to weave the story of God's community, but you are still in the spinning stage, being prepared. We've been carding and spinning, but God is ready to do some serious weaving with you".

Joshua was thinking hard. It was time to take the second spinning, to be born again, to be dyed in the Baptist tradition, to become part of the fabric .

"I've made my commitment," he said to the pastor.

They paused for a moment of prayer.

Timothy: Finding a Place

Hello. My name is Timothy. I would like to share the story of how I came into the Christian church and what it meant to me. It was so important for me as a young man to find a place. My father was a Greek and my mother was a Jew. I was already unsure of my identity when suddenly my mother became a Christian. While I wasn't sure what that meant, it soon became clear that it was very important to her. I found her praying often that my father and I would find Christ, too, whatever that meant. I wasn't sure. I loved both my mother and my father and it had always been important to my father that I be Greek. At his wish I had never been circumcised. What was my place?

Then one day a man named Paul came to Lystra to preach. My mother said he was a great teacher and she took me to meet him. I was overcome by the power of his message, his personality, his God, and I decided to become a Christian and go with him. I also met his travelling companion, Silas, a solid, gracious, likeable man,. I began to feel that I had found my place with them. I was so young, my mother said, and yet Paul and Silas valued me despite my youth. They did not consider me an outsider. They invited me on one preaching mission and then another. I developed a rich prayer and study life as I became a follower of Christ and a worshiper of God. Paul later wrote me a letter in which he encouraged me to let no one despise me because of my youth. He knew that my relationship with God was real.

Paul was an exciting mentor and we were often in and out of trouble, but it was because of him that I came to God and discovered my true identity as a Christian. The church was the home for which I had hungered.

Jitsuo Morikawa, Disciple of a Multicultural Age (1912-1987)

What a moment it was. It was a moment of intense disappointment in his country for the young Japanese American pastor who was taken to the Poston Relocation Center in Arizona for the final eighteen months of the Second World War. It was a moment of racism stemming from public hysteria over the place of Japanese Americans, which denied basic human rights to U.S. citizens. It was a moment of alienation, of fear, of deep despair over the shape of the future. It was a long moment (eighteen months) but the young pastor sensed that it was not an eternal moment; it was a moment that would pass.

What a moment it was. It was a moment of recognition in which the pastor noted the faithfulness and ministry of his own church denomination and of the American Friends Service Committee. It was a moment of spiritual journey and a rebirth of hope. He would characterize this moment forty years later as an American experience comparable to the experience of Joseph in Genesis "whose sale into slavery by his brothers turned to God's purpose" and "brought to the surface the conscience and courage of the church."[1]

Following his experience at Poston, Jitsuo Morikawa decided to test the spiritual power of the church, not only among Asian Americans, but in multicultural settings. A twelve-year ministry at the First Baptist Church of Chicago brought people of many backgrounds and cultures into a major urban renewal program in the Hyde Park-Kenwood community and into the church which sparked it. His burning spiritual quest for ministry to all persons brought him to a ten-year tenure as director of evangelism and then the position of associate executive secretary of the Board of National Ministries of the American Baptist Churches. Following his retirement in 1976, he served as senior interim minister of the multicultural Riverside Church in New York City and finally as pastor of the First Baptist Church of Ann Arbor, Michigan.

Jitsuo Morikawa, throughout his life, understood the public dimensions of sin. He knew that institutions, too, needed to be converted to Christ. He understood not only the power of sin, but the power of God for new life. God would perfect the pattern of God's reign to make a place for all persons. Institutions would also be converted for God's purposes.

Born in British Columbia, Canada, educated in Los Angeles and Louisville, Kentucky, serving God in Rosemead (CA), Poston, Chicago, Philadelphia, New York City, and Ann Arbor, Jitsuo Morikawa became a witness to many as a disciple of Jesus Christ. We share the words of his friend Dr. Paul Nagano who, reflecting on his death, said of him, "Indeed we all rise up to call him blessed."[2]

[1]Adapted from Jitsuo Morikawa, "*The American Baptist Magazine,* vole. 185, no. 6 (Nov.-Dec. 1987), p. 58
[2]Ibid.

Baptists Witness through:

Believer's baptism by immersion

Autonomy of the local church

Primacy of Scripture, and

Two ordinances, baptism and the Lord's Supper, mark our

Interdependent churches

Separating church and state

Trusting in the sufficiency of God's grace (without priests or sacraments)

Serving in lay ministries

Without creeds

Inclusively

To all the world in mission with

New life in Christ

Ecumenically demonstrating

Soul freedom and

Sensitivity to the Holy Spirit.

Baptist Matching Quiz

a. formed a church in Newport, and went to England to secure a charter to form the new colony of Rhode Island.

b. opened a school for young black women in Connecticut prior to the Civil War and was persecuted for her efforts.

c. a poet who worked in a mission hospital in the Philippines and was killed with several other missionaries during World War II.

d. served God in difficult mission projects in South Carolina, Boston, and Burma.

e. a black American who served as a missionary to Liberia in the early nineteenth century.

f. an early missionary who overcame torture, imprisonment, and the loss of two devoted wives to translate the Bible into the Burmese language.

g. lost his life in the midst of a prophetic witness for justice during a sanitation workers' strike in Memphis, Tennessee, in 1968.

h. expelled from Massachusetts because of his conviction about "soul freedom," he founded a new colony in Rhode Island and pastored the first Baptist church in America.

i. an American Indian who overcome ethnic discrimination and personal bitterness to become a pastor and public speaker after the age of fifty.

j. overcame a physical handicap, acquired while working in the "Hell's Kitchen" area of New York City, to become a famous theologian.

1. Roger Williams

2. John Clarke

3. Adoniram Judson

4. Lott Carey

5. Prudence Crandall

6. John Frost

7. Ellen Cushing

8. Walter Rauschenbusch

9. Jennie Clare Adams

10. Martin Luther King, Jr.

Answers to quiz:

9 c	6 i	3 f	
8 j	5 b	2 a	
10 g	7 d	4 e	1 h

83

12

Rewoven for Reweaving

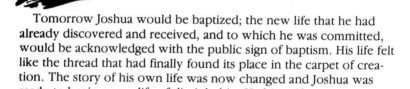

Tomorrow Joshua would be baptized; the new life that he had already discovered and received, and to which he was committed, would be acknowledged with the public sign of baptism. His life felt like the thread that had finally found its place in the carpet of creation. The story of his own life was now changed and Joshua was ready to begin a new life of discipleship. He himself was rewoven by God and was now ready, in God's image, to begin reweaving the rest of the fabric of life in which he was enmeshed. He was tired from the stress of being rewoven and at the same time felt renewed by the opportunity of reweaving his world.

These thoughts tugged at his mind as he climbed the steps of Mrs. Richards' porch and fell heavily into one of the rockers in the ponder place. This porch, the seats by the looms, the place by the creek—all seemed like "holy places" to him now.

"There is a way in which I feel worn out," he was saying to his mentor. "It's like I'm exhausted from a long journey but I haven't really been anywhere."

"Not all the journeys we take in life are out there," Mrs. Richards replied, pointing at the Kansas landscape. "Some of the hardest, the most exhausting, are in here— [she clutched her fist to her chest]—through the landscape of the heart. That journey inside has to take place first; then the journey outside to new life can happen. You've found some friends for your new journey?"

"Yes," Joshua said, "many friends. You and Jessie, George and Ella, and the people at church and the pastor. But there are a lot more—Ruth, Elijah, Esther, Timothy, Peter, Roger Williams, William Carey, Howard Thurman, Will Campbell, Kim Mammaday, Jitsuo Morikawa, Joanna Moore—so many others in my cloud of witness. Somehow the Holy Spirit has brought them all together for me. They have all made Jesus and his gift of life more real and true for me."

"Weave your life with strong threads like those as resources and you will have a strong fabric," said Mrs. Richards. "Let me offer you one more friend. This is a story that my mother told me."

"Jesse Bushyhead was a Cherokee Indian and a Baptist minister, too. Jesse had a strong mind and he became a very learned man, skilled in the English language as well as in the Cherokee. He lived in the first half of the last century when such skill was uncommon. Jesse Bushyhead was one of the writers of the constitution of the Cherokee nation and he served as the 'chief justice' for his people during most of his life. Just before the Cherokee nation was uprooted and sent to the western territories, he spent six months with other tribal leaders in Washington, D.C. They were trying to correct or rewrite a treaty by which an unauthorized group of Cherokees, deceived and lied to, had given up the tribal claim to the land where they had always lived.

"Jesse failed to get the treaty rewritten and the land was lost. The journey of his people west was brutal and deadly, but it must have been no more brutal and deadly than the journey of a sensitive Christian man into the depths of his own heart. How he had failed, he must have thought, even with his good mind, his education, his silver tongue. Had God failed his people as well?

"The inward journey must have been as exhausting as the outward. But he was not defeated; instead, he became strong. You see, it wasn't only a strong mind which Jesse Bushyhead had. There was a warm heart, feeling for the hurts of his people, and a powerful experience of God's Spirit which kept him going in all times of deep disappointment and despair.

"As his own soul grew strong, his body responded. While he had failed at one task, he would not fail at the task of bringing God's Spirit to his people. His deep sense of mission drove him to ride a 240-mile circuit as a pastor in the new lands and to translate many parts of the Bible, including all of Genesis, into the language of his people. Jesse Bushyhead became the spirit thread for that Cherokee part of the fabric that he had been woven to weave. The way he had been woven made Jesse a stronger weaver; the stress of the inward journey made him stronger for the outward journey into discipleship and ministry."

"That's how I want to know God, with all my self and all my life—mind, body, and soul," Joshua responded.

"You will. You're turned in the right direction but there are some other friends that you will need for the journey."

"Who are they?"

"Not 'who' but 'what.' They are the *spiritual disciplines* that will keep you in touch with God, Jesus, and the Holy Spirit. They will make a firm foundation for your mission and ministry out in the world. These are personal prayer, regular and responsible worship with a community of faith, regular Bible study, and an ongoing involvement with a concrete ministry in Christ's name. These are absolutely necessary. Other helpful disciplines are keeping a journal, attending regular spiritual retreats, reading about our Christian and Baptist traditions, and witnessing to others about the new life in Christ."

"It sounds like a lot of work for someone who started out being tired," Josh said.

"I know it sounds that way, but it's the kind of work that renews and refreshes. I can't explain it. I just know it from experience."

Just then the phone rang and Mrs. Richards went to answer it. "It's for you," she called to Josh.

It was Ella. "There is a package here you've been waiting for," she told him. "It's from the adoption agency."

Josh told her that he would be right home and hung up the phone.

"When we were studying with the pastor, we read a story about William Carey, the Baptist missionary," he told Mrs. Richards. "When he went to India, he found out that many missionaries renamed the people whom they baptized with Christian names. Some were Bible names but many of them were just plain old English names like 'Jones.' William Carey didn't approve. He thought that the changed life was more important than something external like a changed name. He encouraged the people to keep their own names which were important in their own families and villages.

"I began to wonder about my name. It's a Bible name from the missionaries, but I didn't even know if I had been given a Navajo name. I asked George and Ella and they didn't know either. They thought it was important, though. They encouraged me to write to the adoption agency to see. I got one letter that said they were researching my history. Maybe this package today will have my name. Then maybe I can decide which one I like best."

"Let me know what it is. I know something about Navajo names," Mrs. Richards said.

"I'd sort of like to choose my own personal name like I've chosen 'Christian' and 'Baptist' as names now," Joshua replied.

Mrs. Richards smiled as she watched him walking up the road toward home, carrying two new names and looking for a third. Her artist's eye, framing his back against the farmhouse, began to consider patterns that might describe the beginning of this exciting new piece of God's fabric.

Peter: The Broken Man Made Whole

Peter and the other disciples were shattered. Not knowing what to do after the terrible death of Jesus, they returned to the activity they knew best—fishing. They weren't doing very well when suddenly someone from the shore called them and told them to cast their nets on the other side of the boat. When the nets filled up, they knew it was Jesus who had called. Peter plunged into the water and rushed to shore.

When they got to shore they found a charcoal fire and frying fish and bread. Jesus fed them. Peter must have been very uncomfortable; it was so recently that he had three times denied knowing Jesus. He was a big, strong fisherman, nicknamed "the rock," who had been broken by his own fear. Now that he had failed Jesus at a crucial time, he wasn't sure if he was good for anything. Jesus, however, was sure.

When they had finished eating, Jesus turned to Peter and asked, "Simon, son of John, do you love me more than these?" Peter replied as evenly and with as much courage as he could muster, "Yes, Lord, you know that I love you." And Jesus said, "Feed my lambs." This exchange of words was repeated twice, and the third time Peter realized that he was being given the opportunity to wipe out his triple failure with triple service. When Jesus then said to him again, "Follow me," Peter knew that he had been reborn for a new life of serving his Lord. The broken man had been made whole for mission.

A Rescued Dream[1]

I remember so clearly the image of those big leather boots suddenly there before me outside the railroad station, penetrating the wall of tears gushing through my eyes. I wiped my eyes and raised them and then raised them some more to the top of a big man, black like me. His words were brief and to the point.

"Boy, what in hell are you crying about?"

I tried to explain the best I could. I blubbered on in too many words about how I was to travel to the Florida Baptist Academy in Jacksonville which was one of the only three high schools for blacks in all of Florida. When I had bought my bus ticket, the man had told me I couldn't carry my old suitcase with me because it didn't have a handle and was only tied shut. It could go freight express, but I didn't have enough money for that. My fear and disappointment had gotten the best of me; I was totally crushed.

Again his words were brief.

"If you're trying to get out of this town to get an education, the least I can do is help. Come with me."

I walked with that big man into the train station where he paid for my bag to go freight express, pulling the necessary coins out of a rawhide bag that he had removed from his belt. I lifted my suitcase to the freight counter to have it marked for Jacksonville. When I turned to say thank you, he was gone. When I ran to the door of the station, I saw a dark figure moving on down the tracks. I wasn't sure if it was the same man who had helped me find the new life I needed.

More than sixty years later when I completed writing my autobiography *With Head and Heart,* a vision of those big boots and that powerful man came to me again and I dedicated that book which held the story of my whole life in its fragile words and pages:

> To the stranger in the railroad station
> in Daytona Beach who restored my broken
> dream sixty-five years ago.

[1] Adapted from Howard Thurman, *With Head and Heart: The Story of Howard Thurman* (New York: Harvest/HBJ Book, 1981).

EPILOGUE:

The Ground of Grace: I Am a Child of God

Dear Jessie,

Your grandmother says that you will be coming to visit in two weeks. I hope that you will save some time for me. There is so much to talk about. Will you be going to the Baptist camp this summer? I am registered for the first week in July. Let me know.

In art class this week we looked at some pictures from the Sistine Chapel by Michelangelo. Have you seen them? I especially like the picture of God reaching toward Adam with a forefinger. Adam is reaching back but not too hard. He is sort of leaning back away from God, taking it easy. The two fingers that should touch just miss. I'm glad our fingers touched out by the creek. I think your hand was the hand of God for an uncertain Adam. My people have always had holy places and that place by the creek seems holy to me now when I go back. The bank of the creek is a kind of firm ground of grace which reminds me that I am a child of God.

I need reminding. I have discovered that the new life still has the old problems. The weaving of my story keeps unraveling or drawing in the wrong strings or featuring the wrong colors. It's all I can do to keep my finger on the spirit thread. Of course, with all the problems, life is really new. There's that added dimension of strength or power with me or within me that does transform the possibilities in everything. Do you feel that way? Somehow I sense this direction. How does it seem to you? Your grandmother keeps telling me that "soul making" is not easy. Maybe my faith is like my school jacket; it's too large now but I'm growing into it.

Remember, call me from your grandmother's house.
Sincerely,
Josh

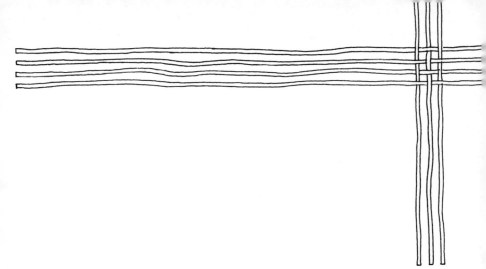

Dear Josh,

What can I say? The gift is beautiful. It was so good to see you again this weekend. Just seeing you helped me to remember all the thinking and struggling that went into making that decision for Christ.

It's good to know that I'm not the only one who has trouble with the new life sometimes. But we are going to make it, aren't we? With some help from our friends? Mrs. Hartley keeps telling me that sometimes what looks like it's unravelling or coming apart from the outside really has some kind of meaning behind it. I hope so. I'm so glad that salvation is by grace through faith. I can't wait to show her this gift.

The gift—I've never had a shawl before. The colors are so rich and meaningful. The grey background suggests the cloudiness or the sadness of so much of the world. The tall tree is like the mysteriousness of God. The clear water is like the cleansing of baptism and the red hands that touch are like the gift of the Spirit (the flame of Pentecost). Am I right? The ground of grace is right here in this pattern for me. It fits together so beautifully. Will I wear it or hang it? I'm not sure.

I remember the day I got baptized. It was like the cold water woke me up out of a dream. The sermon was about Elijah and Elisha and how the prophet's mantle was passed from person to person. The shawl feels like a mantle from my grandmother through you. It is a symbol of the Baptist faith in *Storyweaving*. It will always remind me of a very special moment of faith and it is a picture from which to build my life. The baptism was just the beginning, wasn't it?

I'm glad that we will be going to camp at the same time. It will be good to have a friend I know. Write me soon and let me know what you decide about your new name.

Sincerely,

Jessie

For Further Reading

Bagnull, Marlene, *I Am Special: Prayer Diary for Junior High Girls.* Valley Forge: Judson Press, 1987.

Brown, John, *I've God Mixed-Up Feelings, God.* Valley Forge: Judson Press, 1984.

Bunyan, John, *Pilgrim's Progress.* Many editions.

Campbell, Will D., *Brother to a Dragonfly.* New York: Continuum Press, 1980.

Moore, John Allen, *Anabaptist Portraits.* Scottdale, Pa.: Herald Press, 1948.

Thurman, Howard, *With Head and Heart: The Story of Howard Thurman,* New York: Harcourt, Brace, Jovanovich, 1981.

Weems, Ann, *Family Faith Stories.* Philadelphia: The Westminster Press, 1985.

American Baptists: a People of Faith and *American Baptists: A People of Mission.* Pamphlets available from the Office of Communication, American Baptist Churches, U.S.A., P.O. Box 851, Valley Forge, PA 19482-0851.

About Being Baptist. Scriptographic booklet available from Judson Sales, P.O. Box 851, Valley Forge, PA 19482-0851. (Produced by Channing L. Bete Co., Inc., South Deerfield, MA.)

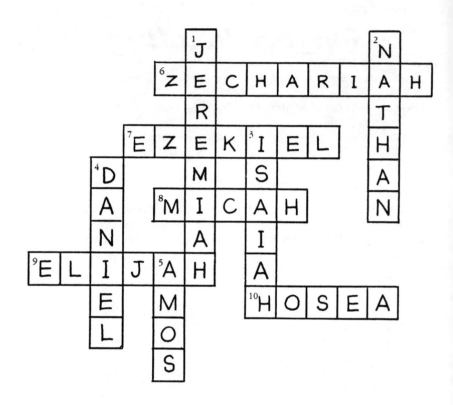

Answer to Care Word Search

share, care, carry, time, hands, drive, attitude, self, you, love, garden, tutor, bread (read), befriend, contribute, cash, help, clothes, rake, shovel, smile, feed, energy, lift

S	H	A	R	E	B	R	O	C	A	R	E
C	A	L	O	N	D	S	H	O	V	E	L
A	N	A	G	A	R	D	E	N	E	A	O
R	D	T	L	I	F	T	N	T	M	C	V
R	S	T	S	M	I	L	E	R	A	K	E
Y	O	I	T	B	E	F	R	I	E	N	D
T	U	T	O	R	U	E	G	B	I	O	E
I	E	U	F	E	E	D	Y	U	A	B	E
M	O	D	E	A	C	L	O	T	H	E	S
E	F	E	N	D	A	L	U	E	E	T	L
B	O	R	D	F	S	E	L	F	L	A	B
D	R	I	V	E	H	I	C	K	P	O	N

95

Answer to Baptist Name Find

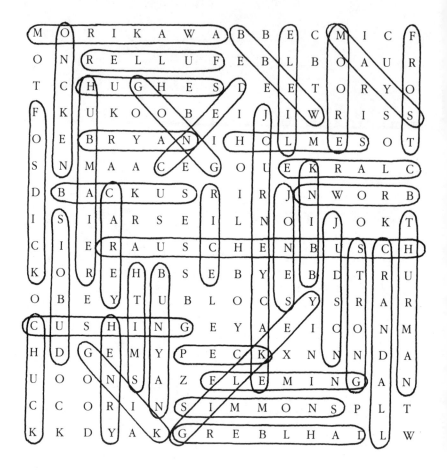

The Judson Church Membership/Discipleship Resources were prepared in part through the use of funds provided by the George Dana and Ella C. Boardman Grant of Educational Ministries, ABC/USA. George Dana Boardman authored a booklet, *The Problem of Jesus,* which is available upon request from:

Judson Press
P.O. Box 851
Valley Forge, PA 19482-0851